Essays on Walter Prescott Webb

The Walter Prescott Webb Memorial Lectures: X
Sponsored by The University of Texas at Arlington

The Walter Prescott Webb Memorial Lectures

Essays on Walter Prescott Webb

By

Joe B. Frantz

W. Turrentine Jackson

W. Eugene Hollon

George Wolfskill

Walter Rundell, Jr.

Foreword by Jubal R. Parten
Introduction by Ray Allen Billington
Edited by Kenneth R. Philp and Elliott West

University of Texas Press   Austin & London

Library of Congress Cataloging in Publication Data
Main entry under title:
Essays on Walter Prescott Webb
    (The Walter Prescott Webb memorial lectures; 10 ISSN 0083-713X)
    1. Webb, Walter Prescott, 1888–1963—Addresses, essays, lectures.
2. Frontier thesis—Addresses, essays, lectures. I. Webb, Walter
Prescott, 1888–1963. II. Frantz, Joe Bertram, 1917–   III. Philp,
Kenneth R., 1941–   IV. West, Elliott, 1945–   V. Series: The
Walter Prescott Webb memorial lectures; 10.
E175.5.W4E77   907'.2'024   75-37672
ISBN 0-292-72016-5

To Robert L. Williamson

Contents

Foreword

It is a distinct privilege to record some of my personal views of the late Walter Prescott Webb. I also wish to congratulate the History Department at the University of Texas at Arlington for the annual series of lectures in memory of this outstanding man, thought by many to be the greatest historian ever to have come out of Texas.

Although my student years at the University of Texas at Austin (1913–1917) coincided with his, I did not have the good fortune to know Webb as a student. During the depression years I spent a great deal of time, as did most oilmen, in an effort to hammer out conservation laws and regulations to eliminate waste in the production and use of oil and gas. During a discussion with my friend the distinguished Dr. Frederic Duncalf in 1933, he suggested, "You should meet and talk to Walter Webb." A few days later he introduced me to Dr. Webb, and thus began one of the most valued friendships of my life.

I realized at once that I had met a real conservationist and intellectual, an individual who fully grasped the purpose of conserving our natural resources for posterity. Webb loved the land, as evidenced in his monograph *Flat Top: A Story of Modern Ranching*. He strongly believed that we should use the land with care and should condition it for continuous production. He and I thoroughly agreed, for instance, that the storage of crude oil in earthen pits was a wanton waste, a practice soon thereafter prohibited by the Railroad Commission of Texas.

Webb was a man of great loyalty to the University of Texas and his colleagues on the faculty. But he was not blind to their weakness and inefficiency, and he often exploded at the appearance of either. As a teacher, he was deeply concerned that the student be exposed to the best teaching from the standpoint of both quality and content. He often criticized administrators, but his were constructive criticisms. No faculty member of his time put forth more effort for improvements in both academic programs and resources.

One of his most significant contributions was his prophetic vision. Traces of this can be found in his important works, from *The Great Plains* through *Divided We Stand*, and it comes to full flower in *The Great Frontier*. It is in *The Great Frontier* that Webb the historian, the scholar, and the prophet twenty-five years ago presented us with his brilliant comprehension of the world we are living in today.

Perhaps a few of Webb's observations in the concluding chapter of *The Great Frontier* (Austin: University of Texas Press, 1964) will illustrate what I mean:

Society as it thickens will become more closely integrated and its members more interdependent. . . . There will be a tendency toward socialization as now exhibited in the United States and Great Britain or toward absolutism as exhibited by the fascist states and by Russia. . . . The individual will become relatively less important and will tend to lose his identity in a growing corporate life. . . . Famine will continue to afflict overpopulated countries . . . (P. 415)

Webb's final observation in *The Great Frontier* deserves our particular attention:

The question before us now is whether we can manage what we have so eagerly taken. That is our challenge and our opportunity. We should not be so obtuse as to believe that the means of management are the same as those of conquest, or that frontier institutions will necessarily serve a metropolitan society. Our challenge consists in finding out what modifications should be made, and our opportunity will come in making them. Our inspiration may come from history, in looking back to the early sixteenth century when the lamp was lifted beside the golden door of the Great Frontier to change the destiny of mankind. (P. 418)

Jubal R. Parten

Preface

On April 3, 1975, the tenth annual Walter Prescott Webb Memorial Lectures were held at the University of Texas at Arlington. To mark the tenth occurrence of the lectures, the speakers, all of whom studied under Professor Webb, examined various aspects of Webb and his ideas.

Webb's southern origins and his ideas on the South as an economic colony of the northeast are discussed by Professor Joe B. Frantz of the University of Texas at Austin. Heeding Webb's call for more attention to comparative frontier studies, Professor W. Turrentine Jackson of the University of California, Davis, reveals how Australian historians have examined the place of the frontier in their own national life and how they have tried to place this experience in an international context. He includes a helpful bibliographical essay on the scholarly literature of comparative frontiers.

Professor W. Eugene Hollon of the University of Toledo takes a contemporary look at Webb's arid-land thesis—that civilization in the desert and mountain West, and indeed human life everywhere, is shaped and limited by geography and available resources. Professor George Wolfskill of the University of Texas at Arlington describes how international law evolved as European mercantilist nations competed for the riches offered by what Webb called "the great frontier" of the New World. The decline of such economic opportunities, he suggests, began a time of turmoil and transition in international law from which we have not yet emerged.

In 1975, the University of Texas at Arlington sponsored its first Webb-Smith essay competition. Funded by a generous grant from C. B. Smith of Austin, the award will be given each year for the best paper submitted on the topic of the lectures. The 1975 winner was Professor Walter Rundell, Jr., of the University of Maryland, whose "Webb the Schoolteacher" examines Professor Webb's educational career prior to his appointment to the faculty of the University of Texas. Professor Rundell's essay is included with the papers delivered during the lectures.

As usual, the Webb Lectures Committee would like to thank all participants in the series—speakers, students, faculty, and the staff of the Press—for their help and cooperation.

This volume is dedicated to the memory of Robert L. Williamson, associate professor of history at the University of Texas at Arlington, who died May 21, 1975. Born in Cleveland, Texas, Bob studied at the University of Texas at Austin under Walter Prescott Webb and taught in Cleveland and Baytown, Texas, before coming to Arlington in 1963. From the first he was an enthusiastic supporter of the Webb Lectures, and he contributed "The Muzzle-Loading Rifle: Frontier Tool" to the third volume of the series. A superb teacher, a grand teller of tales, a good and understanding friend, and a truly decent man, Bob Williamson will remain a personal and professional inspiration to the scores of colleagues and hundreds of students privileged to know and love him.

Kenneth R. Philp
Elliott West

Introduction

Walter Prescott Webb would have thoroughly enjoyed hearing the lectures that have been assembled in this book. He would have been pleased, naturally, that the series of Walter Prescott Webb Memorial Lectures at the University of Texas at Arlington has attracted eminent scholars as speakers and enthusiastic audiences as listeners for a decade. He would have been flattered that most of those lecturers, in 1975 as in prior years, have seen fit to pay tribute to his own contributions and to inquire into the reasons for his own eminence as a historian. But above all, he would have gloried in the fact that scholars have been expanding the trails that he had blazed and that their discoveries are still enriching our knowledge of the nation's—and the world's—past.

For Walter Webb saw the study and writing of history, not solely as an academic exercise, but also as a panacea for the ills of society. History to him was not only an essential ingredient in the training of good citizens and the education of cultured men; it was also—and more importantly—an instrument for social change that could, when properly used, better mankind's lot. Webb saw, and used, history as a weapon, as dangerous as an atomic bomb when employed falsely to sustain dictatorships or imperialistic policies but as potentially useful as safe nuclear energy when directed toward betterment of life for the masses.

His faith in the function of history as an irresistible persuader was shown especially on two occasions. During the 1930s he was shocked to read that the Supreme Court had invalidated a New Deal agency that he viewed as a valuable instrument in the effort to emerge from the Great Depression: the National Recovery Administration. That very night he cast aside other tasks to begin work on a book of protest that would summon facts from the past to prove the court wrong. The harsh little volume that resulted, *Divided We Stand*, was good history, but it was also a masterful brief against government for the few and a convincing argument for the economic rejuvenation of the South as a step toward national recovery. Here spoke Webb the Crusader, his weapon historical truths, logically arranged to present a case for the people against selfish corporate might. To weigh the influence of such a book is impossible, but there can be no question that it did stir controversy, arouse passionate rebuttals, and help convince President Franklin D. Roosevelt to view the South as the nation's most pressing economic problem.

A generation later, in 1963, when Walter Webb was approaching the end of his life, he decided that the mounting racial crisis in the South threatened the progress that his earlier writing had helped make possible. Again he reacted passionately. This time he withdrew as author of a volume in the prestigious New American Nation Series to begin work on a book that would convince southerners that their continued economic well-being would be threatened if they became entangled in the racial struggle. Once more Webb fell back on the arsenal of the past in his battle for a better future. No scholar could pay higher tribute to the persuasive power of historical writing than this. "I wanted to write," he told his fellow craftsmen on one occasion, "so that people could understand me; I wanted to persuade them, lure them along from sentence to paragraph, make them see patterns of truth in the kaleidoscope of the past, exercise upon them the marvelous magic of words as conveyors of thought." Walter Webb was no armchair historian, content to retreat from the world. He was an evangelist, preaching the gospel from the mountaintop and guiding mankind along the road to salvation.

So it is that he would read the pages of this book with excited approval. And well he might, for the five historians who have contributed to the volume have written essays that he would have found challenging, not simply because they contain sound history, well expressed, but also because they reveal his own impact on later scholarship. These essays develop themes that Webb himself suggested, and, by doing so, they push back the borders of knowledge a bit farther.

Two of the essayists, Walter Rundell, Jr., and Joe B. Frantz, have chosen to focus on Walter Webb's own career. Walter Rundell's detail-packed study of Webb's early life provides us with a preview of one portion of the biography on which he is engaged. In it he explores Walter Webb's early career to reveal "those elements in his experiences as a schoolteacher that foreshadowed or contributed to his intellectual maturation." It is a story with a vast array of information on Webb's high school teaching and the rigors of life in the small-town Texas of that day. Today's reader emerges with a better understanding of the genesis of Webb's social philosophy, as well as a vast admiration for the energy and ambition that allowed him to rise above his humble beginnings.

Joe B. Frantz, a long-time colleague and close friend of Walter Webb, draws on his personal experiences as well as a careful reading of Webb's works in his examination of the influence of Webb's southern upbringing, education, and prejudices on his historical beliefs. By doing so he demonstrates convincingly that Webb was basically a southern Populist, but with views modified by his years in West Texas, where western influences partially counterbalanced those acquired during his formative years in East Texas. He emerged as an "evangelist for the South," preaching the need for a strengthened economy that would lessen dependence on the North and urging his fellow southerners to shun involvement in racial conflicts to allow economic progress to go on unchecked. Frantz believes that Webb's death in

1963 may possibly have been "another in a long list of southern tragedies."

Each of the remaining three essayists has chosen to explore a theme suggested in Walter Webb's own works, building on the foundations he laid to extend and deepen our knowledge of the American experience. One, W. Eugene Hollon, has elected to use Webb's *The Great Plains* as his starting point; the others, W. Turrentine Jackson and George Wolfskill, find their inspiration in *The Great Frontier*.

Hollon's stimulating essay tells us something of Webb's indoctrination into plains life and more about the genesis of his books and articles on the subject; it then sets out to up-date Webb's thesis that "the amount of moisture available for the entire Great Plains could not support large oasis cities and irrigation indefinitely." Using modern statistics, Hollon paints a terrifying picture of the current depletion of the plains' resources—a picture that casts Webb in the role of an uncomfortably accurate prophet. Walter Webb would have enjoyed Gene Hollon's conclusions; he would have appreciated even more that the boosters who damned him for branding the plains country a "desert" were beginning by the 1970s to acknowledge that he was perfectly right. The picture that Professor Hollon paints—of unregulated growth, of increasingly depleted water supplies, of the ravaging of the plains' fragile environment—is well worth reading and heeding. His gloomy conclusion—"there simply is not enough water in the arid West to supply the growing cities, new energy plants, strip-mining operations, and irrigation farming"—substantiates Webb's predictions and demonstrates Webb's soundness as an interpretative historian.

Webb's plea that scholars study comparative frontiers as a device for understanding our own provided the inspiration for W. Turrentine Jackson's revealing comparison of the Australian and American frontiers. When Webb's *The Great Frontier* first urged such a study in 1952, the historical profession was too busy castigating the then-discredited "frontier school" of interpretation to accept the invitation. More recently, scholars have awakened to his challenge and have begun comparative studies of major significance. Their findings are admirably summarized by Professor Jackson, who has added new insights of his own. In a series of thoughtful analyses, he contrasts the frontiering experiences of the two countries in terms of mining, treatment of native peoples, agricultural techniques, and, particularly, land policy, the latter especially contributing a great deal to our knowledge. Again his findings prove the correctness of Walter Webb's predictions; Professor Jackson's essay reveals the American frontier in a new and very important light.

The contribution of George Wolfskill, the sole representative of the host institution, ranges farther afield, but provides a brilliant example of the manner in which Webb's germinal ideas have stirred thought and investigation. Basing his argument on the hypothesis of Webb's *The Great Frontier*, Wolfskill states that until the twentieth century the spirit underlying international law had been maintained first by the power of imperial Rome, then by the moral imperative of the Roman Catholic church, and finally by the interrelated and interdependent capitalistic societies that emerged following the Age of Discovery. The end of Webb's "boom period" during the early twentieth century, Wolfskill believes, underlay the intrusion of statism into the hitherto sacred domain of private global economic controls. This in turn outmoded traditional international law as an instrument for world cooperation; that law had developed to protect individual freedoms from state authority, but state usurpation of the role of the individual now robbed it of its original purpose. Global cooperation, he suggests, will be possible only if an alteration in world society comparable to that effected by the New World discoveries demands a renewed expression of international unity. He sees the possibility of such a force in the need for laws governing space exploration and exploitation. Professor Wolfskill's bold reasoning and imaginative conclusions would have charmed Dr. Webb, as they will today's readers.

These essays, then, are a fitting tribute to the man whose name they honor. They explore unfamiliar terrain, are based on solid research, disdain petty pedantry in favor of sound speculation, apply interdisciplinary tools to the problems they seek to solve, and reach conclusions that are usable in bettering the world in which we live. This is the sort of history that Walter Prescott Webb himself wrote.

Ray Allen Billington

Essays on Walter Prescott Webb

Walter Prescott Webb and the South

Joe B. Frantz

"Where do I begin?" That question furnished an opening line for the song wrapped around Erich Segal's runaway best seller of several years ago. It fits here. Where *did* Walter Prescott Webb begin, insofar as the South is concerned? While I am not a devotee of psychohistory, I do feel that at least three possible formative moments reveal the beginning of Webb's southern perceptions.

The first memory of the Civil War of Casner P. Webb, then a small tad, remained vivid all his life. He did not remember whether the scene occurred during the war or after. Trained by parents, neighbors, and events to hate Yankees, he remembered a soldier in blue walking alongside him down a Mississippi mud road, offering him some candy or other sweetmeat. He recalled how desperately he wanted candy, which he had not tasted in some time. On the other hand, he knew that soldiers in blue poisoned little Confederate boys and that he dared not take a chance on the soldier's gift. So the two slogged alongside, the soldier evidently genuinely generous and the boy using all the curse words that a kid can know and meanwhile crying because of his frustration compounded of desire, fear, and dislike. This was the soldier who burned down your home and killed your uncles and threatened unspeakable acts against your mother and sisters and girl cousins.

Decades later, after Casner had died as an old man in Weatherford, Texas, his son Walter picked up the story and told it with some frequency until he in turn was killed in 1963. Although Walter Webb did not hate Yankee soldiers and could place his father's story in some perspective, nonetheless he savored it and undoubtedly it influenced him.

A second indoctrination. Walter Prescott Webb was born on April 3, 1888, on a farm in Panola County in deep East Texas, nestled against the Louisiana line. East Texas has been described as a continuation of the Old South without its mildew. Like any borderland, it treasured its inheritance, which became a form of southern nationalism. In a gentler sense Webb came from the same sort of nationalistic situation in which Austria provided Germany with its rampant nationalist, Adolf Hitler, Corsica gave Napoleon to the French, and Georgia gave Joseph Stalin to Russia. East Texas is only now outgrowing the pleasure of refighting the Civil War. In 1888, in the home of Casner P. and Mary Elizabeth Kyle Webb, the late unpleasantness was undoubtedly real and contemporary. If Casner did not dwell on the perfidy of the Yankees, his neighbors would have.

Webb was married on September 16, 1916, to Jane Elizabeth Oliphant. Her father, a militant southern gentleman, lived with the Webbs until his death, and Mrs. Webb and her daughter were equally militant members of the United Daughters of the Confederacy. They had a strong southern tradition, and Webb used to wonder aloud to intimates whether he had sufficient pedigree to enter the south gate of heaven. In such a situation many men would have rejected all things southern, but could Webb have been brainwashed?

He always seemed to arrive late at everything, and the summer of

1920 found him as a thirty-two–year–old beginning graduate student at the University of Chicago. There he took a course from William E. Dodd called "The Planter in Politics." Webb saved his lecture notes, and they are suggestive and illuminating. Evidently Dodd delivered extremely organized lectures. The very first notes in the class start off with "Class Purpose." Read what Webb took from a professor whom he admired extravagantly:

1. Purpose *of Lecture, to set forth the political institutions and the political practices by which a small group of Southern leaders controlled their own states, to show how, through their unified action, they dominated in the nation for 15 or 20 years before the Civil War, in Congress, the presidency, and the S. C. [Supreme Court].*
2. *I shall proceed by examining their governmental machinery, and their method of operating that machinery in their own interests. By governmental machinery, I mean, of course, their institutions.*
   The fundamental institutions of the South are the County and its offices, and the Parish and its offices. None of these institutions are indigenous to American soil. They come [sic] *over, along with the furniture, in the Mayflower. They are English institutions transferred to the American colonists.*[1]

Farther into the notes is a paragraph of quotations from the autobiography of the Wisconsin progressive reformer Robert La Follette (incidentally Webb misspelled the name as La Follett). Webb did not indicate whether this was something he had read or an excerpt from Dodd's lecture, but, since he copied the paragraph *in toto*, we have to believe it came from the La Follette book:

We have long rested comfortably in this country upon the assumption that because our form of government was democratic, it was therefore automatically producing democratic results. Now there is nothing mysteriously potent about the forms and names of democratic institutions that should make them self operative. Tyranny and oppression are just as operative under democratic forms as under any other. We are slow to realize that democracy is a life; and involves continual struggle. It is only as those of every generation who love democracy resist with all their might the encroachment of its en-

emies that the idea of representative government can even be approximated.[2]

However it began, Webb's feeling for the South as a creature of imposed institutions took hold. He grew up with a southern father and mother, married a southern-thinking girl and had an equally southern-thinking daughter, housed his southern gentleman of a father-in-law in his own home, took courses in southern history with a compelling professor with traditional feelings about the South, and lived in communities that were at least peripherally southern.

Almost the same story could be outlined about orthodox religion. Among Webb's own earliest memories was sleeping on a quilt spread on the floor or ground at protracted meetings and revivals with the long skirts of the women swishing across his half-asleep body as they made their way up to the altar to confess their sins. But he early separated himself from regular religious interests and took little notice of religion during most of the remainder of his life.

For him orthodox Christianity did not quite represent the unanimity of experience and surroundings as did the religion of southernism. His father, whom he never felt he could please and always believed he disappointed by becoming a teacher and writer, was, in the parlance of Webb's youth, a scoffer, and most of the contention between Casner P. and Mary Kyle Webb derived from his denigration of her pious religious beliefs. But no one whom he admired as much as his father appeared to teach him to scoff at southern myths and deceptions.

Webb grew up in West Texas as a marginal plainsman who liked to say to strangers who would ask him when he first began to work on his book *The Great Plains*, "When I was four," or some other such seemingly flippant answer. If a questioner pressed him, Webb would explain seriously that watching a southern farmer try to ply his craft on the dry flats of West Texas had opened the eyes of Webb the boy to all the special conditions of the treeless, arid plains. He grew up a young plainsman, and spiritually he never left the plains.

At the same time Webb absorbed a considerable amount of populist ideas. He was twelve years old when the twentieth century began, and though populism had declined by then its true believers remained numerous and as vehement as ever about how they were being taken by "the interests." The railroad was still a prime enemy in Texas, the progressivism of Theodore Roosevelt and others was just shifting into high gear, and Texas insurgents sought to throw out absentee owners of companies doing business in their state. The tradition of Jim Hogg spread over the state like a blanket, and the Waters-Pierce Oil Company was driven from the state for violating state laws. On the national level Judge Kennesaw Mountain Landis fined Standard Oil $29 million for violating antitrust statutes, and in Webb's twenty-third year the Supreme Court of the United States broke Standard Oil into fragments. To a sensitive lad the implications were obvious: you could not trust a northern corporation, which would skin you alive or try to put itself above the law.

This popular attitude has an enduring base. Ralph Yarborough, who held one of the longer tenures as a United States senator from Texas, sprang from the deep East Texas soil. He could always depend on carrying East Texas, although his racial views ran counter to those of his neighbors and some of his economic views provoked alarm. East Texas never wavered in its support of Yarborough because he fought the interests. Those interests could be robed as the *Dallas Morning News* or as Texas oilmen, but the senator projected for his constituents a picture of taking on the big boys wherever they might be, whether in some nebulous place called Wall Street or in the big Texas cities like Houston and Dallas. And, as they trooped to the polls, East Texans would say, "Ralph has gone overboard for the Negroes, but one thing is sure, he'll fight the interests." And they would vote for Ralph as their David to fight the Goliath of big-business power.

Webb was only eight years old when William Jennings Bryan came out of the West in 1896 to lead a people's crusade against the Republican party and its handmaiden, the business interests. But, in an era when a farm boy had little to do afterhours except listen to his elders ruminate and argue, he would have heard his litigious-minded father and his neighbors talk about the defeat of the poor man's candidate, and he was twelve and twenty years old when an older Bryan ran the next two times. He would have seen the triumph of wealth and organization over a man with little to offer except cheaper money and heart. He might have felt, as his slightly older contemporaries did, that Bryan's defeats represented the last stand of small-town and rural America against an all-powerful industrial machine.

But he would have been sidetracked with getting an education, trying his hand at writing, marrying and starting a family, and somehow making a living. There was little time for fighting.

By 1931 he was established. His *The Great Plains* received enough of an admixture of favorable and unfavorable reactions to build a proper scar tissue against the needles of criticism. He would have felt that surge of faith in himself that enables a writer to continue sticking out his neck, knowing that, once he publishes an opinion, it belongs to the public and no longer to himself and that this orphan child he has turned loose is likely to get hacked beyond recognition.

Webb's next book was safe, a local work on the Texas Rangers, which established him in Texas as one of the state's most prominent historians. Although *The Great Plains* was a better book, it attracted scholars and thinkers, a category that did not include most Texans, even those who read. But during the depression Webb sold *The Texas Rangers* to the movies for real money, and that made Texans notice him. Hollywood only used the title, but Texans turned out to see Jack Oakie cavort in a movie that they thought was written about them by one of their own. Webb had become a Texas name.

Webb did not work well under anyone's compulsion except his own. He could waste time as well as any person, although it is debatable whether all his reading and talking and thinking were really a waste of time. When he contracted to someone else to write a book, the manuscript was such a burden that he later took a vow never to accept an advance. He failed to keep that vow, but he turned down more advances than he accepted. He liked to say that, after he had been given an advance by a publisher, he had no inducement to do work for which he had already been paid.

Divided We Stand was not a book for which he had an advance. Not at all. Instead, it developed the way he liked his books to grow. To him the New Deal represented a reincarnation and culmination of the aspirations of Bryan and his followers. Franklin D. Roosevelt was Bryan removed a third of a century further, except that Roosevelt was successful. The new president had consulted with the country's frightened leaders and had led them into using the power of the government to distribute whatever blessings remained in this nation to the poor rather than to the mighty. In Webb's eyes, Roosevelt was reversing the nineteenth-century governmental process of taking from the many and giving to the few. Webb believed this procedure was the proper function of the American dream.

But then the Supreme Court, composed of holdovers from an earlier, less experimental age, began to rule against New Deal measures —the National Recovery Administration and the Agricultural Adjustment Administration, in particular. When the Supreme Court declared the AAA unconstitutional, the decision caught Webb in a rebellious mood. To him, here was the first administration in his lifetime that had really tried to transform the United States into a great democratic nation, but snipers were picking off its best efforts. At almost white heat Webb went to work.

His manuscript became a crusade. Though one historian, way off in Texas, could do little to turn the country around, he refused to go down without fighting. Franklin D. Roosevelt led his troops, the American people, into a third American revolution, and in the election of 1936 the people had ratified the turnaround. But now the Supreme Court was proving that its legal and intellectual will reigned supreme over the collective will of those same people. Webb concluded that the Supreme Court's decisions represented a return to rule by economic royalists.

The more Webb thought and wrote, the angrier he became. He divided the nation into three parts: a South, which included Texas; a West, which followed the eastern boundaries of Oklahoma to North Dakota; and the North. He buttressed his argument with census figures, and he proved to his satisfaction how the North dominated the nation and acted as a sort of feudal lord to the other two sections. The story that he developed told of what the North had done *for* or *to* the other sections, but the "done to" far outweighed the "done for."

What Webb prepared was not so much a historical narrative as an exceptional brief for the prosecution. He quoted Abbott Lawrence on the Tariff of 1828 as saying, "This bill if adopted as amended will keep the South and West in debt to New England the next hundred years." When Webb repeated Lawrence's statement, originally written to Daniel Webster, he placed the entire sentence in italics. He then asserted not only that Lawrence was correct in his estimate but also that, a hundred years "and almost a decade to boot" later, "the South and West are still in debt to the North, more deeply than they were in 1828."

The book hit hard. It cited examples of corporate forays into the South and West and accused the North of depleting southern and western capital and of taking more out than it put in. He felt that the South and West were in continual economic vassalage to the North. For example, more than ten million cars were registered in the two sections, and yet every one of them came from one of three or four manufacturers in the North. The ultimate profits and the labor benefits "flowed to the North." If owners purchased their cars on time, interest charges went to pay a northern insurance company. Meanwhile, like good vassals, the men in the service departments of the local automobile companies and the men at the service stations wore the uniform of the northern company they served. The men were told what to sell and how to sell it, and they represented a degree of regimentation of which the vassals themselves were not always conscious.

Between 90 and 95 percent of national advertising originated in the North (that was before the advent of Colonel Sanders' Kentucky Fried Chicken!), while, of 4,664 firms making or selling drug supplies, 3,948 were in the North. Ninety-five percent of the $105 billion of insurance was in the hands of northern companies.

Almost every page was quotable. And best of all, from an author's standpoint, the book was taken seriously. One review called it good and necessary and overdue, and the next accused it of being a destructive pamphlet that ignored the North's contributions toward development in the other two sections.[3] Webb felt that the book partially explained President Roosevelt's following through on his own statement that the South was the nation's No. 1 economic problem. In later years, when the South boomed, partly from the attention it had received from the federal government, Webb felt that in some degree he was responsible.

Divided We Stand also brought out a bit of the martyr complex that inhabits the souls of most writers. As Webb said in his essay "History as High Adventure":

> Divided We Stand *guaranteed that I would never be called to a Northern university. . . . The book has been called a pamphlet, a philippic, and a good many other things. Because the people could read it and did, it was not objective. . . . It explained how, after the Civil War, the North, directed by the Republican party, seized eco-*

nomic control of the nation and maintained it through corporate mo-
nopoly. The result was that by 1930 the North, with 21 per cent of
the territory and 57 per cent of the people, owned and controlled ap-
proximately 85 per cent of the nation's wealth, although about 90
per cent of the natural resources were located in the South and West.
. . . The book in original form trod on the toes of a powerful monop-
oly of patents, and it in turn trod on my publisher, leading to expur-
gation in galley of all reference to this company and to its products,
glass bottles. The book was quickly declared out of print on the ground
that it did not sell.

But it had done its work. The Hartford Empire Company was
hauled to Washington, where I saw the same men who had dictated
virtually what I should print about milk bottles quail before Thur-
man Arnold's young attorneys, who gave an examination that Hart-
ford Empire did not pass. . . .

Although declared out of print, the book would not die. The federal
investigation of the Hartford Empire Company put all the records in
the public domain. From these records I told the whole story and pub-
lished the revised book myself. It is now in the fourth edition, has
sold 15,000 copies, and is still in print. The original publisher is out
of business.[4]

As most Webb aficionados know, *Divided We Stand* continues in pa-
perback and is still sold and read. Although some of its statistics have
been updated, the main thesis has needed little change.

Webb waited fifteen years to publish his next book, *The Great Frontier*, which expanded his viewpoint from the regional and national to
that of the world. With the way the world economy has been changing lately, *The Great Frontier* is being re-examined for its somewhat
gloomy prophecies that the boom days are past, and Webb may stand
on the threshold of being hailed as a major prophet. No less a syndi-
cated column than that of *Mother Earth News* so dubbed him recently.

Webb also took time to write for the *Southwest Review* an article,
"How the Republican Party Lost Its Future," which was republished
with some frequency and was given a three-column analysis by *Time*
magazine. Unlike most of Webb's ideas, which caught on slowly but
surely, this article became an immediate success, only to have the
election of Dwight D. Eisenhower as president for two terms in the

1950s prove it wrong.

But that is not part of our story. While Webb formulated his ideas for *The Great Frontier*, he also brooded about *Divided We Stand*. Accordingly he re-examined his figures to see what changes had occurred between 1930 and 1950. In every category of wealth and well-being, he found, his two vassal sections had gained, sometimes spectacularly, while the North, still leading, had lost comparatively. Two Texans presided over the national House of Representatives and the Senate. Webb, no sports fan, also believed it important that even sports were pushing westward—the New York Giants and the Brooklyn Dodgers were now the San Francisco Giants and the Los Angeles Dodgers.

More important, this re-examination also renewed Webb's interests in the South. An invitation to give the Fleming Lectures at Louisiana State University at Baton Rouge turned his thoughts toward the region. In examining the newest South, Webb found a welcome change from the gloom that he often provoked. Here, glory be, was "a cheering story." He had traveled across the South, and his reporter's eye saw improved conditions. "I saw fat cattle on green meadows, better farms and crops, and fresh paint on houses. I saw Southerners wearing good clothes, registering in the best hotels, carrying themselves with confidence into banks and business houses and coming out with what they went in for. They walked a little taller, and they found something in their pockets besides their empty hands."[5]

But this was a feeling, an opinion, that had nothing to do with history or with fact, only with what Webb felt. He needed proof.

So Webb took out his measuring stick and examined, and the pessimism expressed in *Divided We Stand* turned to excitement. The statistics bore him out. Without going into all their ramifications, consider that in those twenty years the "Northern individual's income had increased 119 per cent; the Westerner's had increased 148 per cent; but the Southerner's had increased 223 per cent."[6]

The South had been rediscovered, but Webb gave politics a limited amount of credit in this improvement. He began to look at the South as a piece of real estate in which to put one's money. As always, Webb enumerated:

1. *The South is the only region in the United States that fronts the sea on two sides.*
2. *The South has one-third of the good farm land in the nation and the land is getting better every year.*
3. *The South has two-thirds of all the land in the nation with forty inches of rainfall or more.*
4. *The South has a long growing season, and is the richest region in renewable resources. It is again becoming a great forest.*
5. *The interior South has the greatest supply of fresh water in the nation, exclusive of the Great Lakes.*
6. *The South produces 45 per cent of the oil, most of the sulphur, and has enormous deposits of coal and iron which have hardly been touched.*[7]

In short, the South was the region richest in natural resources and with the greatest potential. Webb believed the time had come to start investing in the South. Fate, technology, and the Lord, according to Webb, had come over to the South's side, and he welcomed all three of them.

Webb became an evangelist for the South. He disposed of the region's historic handicaps as no longer valid, and he tried to dismiss southern reluctance to change. He made speeches on the future of the South wherever he could get an audience. With a certain airiness he told southerners that they ought to face up to the racial question by ignoring it and suggested that, if both black and white races could get disgustingly rich, they could live in harmony. He liked to use Abraham Lincoln's comparison of Brigham Young to a hickory tree that had fallen across the field he was plowing. The tree was too heavy to move and too green to burn, Lincoln supposedly reasoned, so he just plowed around it, and he would do the same with Brigham Young.

Webb's suggestion in the late 1950s that the South plow around the racial question did not always meet with favor in parts of the Deep South. James W. Silver, chairman of the Department of History at the University of Mississippi, was asked by some of the university's board to resign as chairman for showing such poor judgment as to invite that dangerous Texas radical to their school.

Webb envisioned a series of South-wide conferences where professors, businessmen, and students would carry the torch for the South.

After they had evangelized for about a year, he hoped to call together all southern governors and persuade them to unite in presenting a case to their respective legislatures to accelerate the momentum in upgrading the South. As he said, he felt nothing heroic in singing "I'll live and die in Dixie." Since he hated poverty and loved life, he observed, he would rather say, "Let's live—and prosper—in Dixie."[8]

Personal involvements prevented Webb from implementing his ideas. After his first wife died, he began to spend a large amount of time getting his own fairly considerable estate in shape, he romanced and married Terrell Maverick, and he collaborated with her in editing a book, *Washington Wife*, which hit the national best-seller lists briefly. As he told me, "If it sells 40,000 copies, I'm going to buy an Oldsmobile." He was still driving Plymouths when he was killed in a one-car accident.

Briefly, this is the story of Webb and the South. Always a promoter, he wound up praising the South as the great underdeveloped area of the nation that could only be defeated by itself. To him, his own life provided inspiration for the South. Webb had been born of parents who had left Mississippi "to escape the poverty . . . imposed upon them by the Civil War and its aftermath." He wrote, "They brought their poverty to Texas with them, along with a lot of bitter stories, and I grew up on both." Though they gradually escaped poverty, Webb never escaped the stories. "Their influence was such as to make me turn away from Southern history to the less tragic and more rambunctious story of the American West."[9]

But in the end he came full circle and returned to a renewed examination of the land of his fathers. If he had survived a few more years, who can say what he might have got underway.

But he did not, and we are left with an incomplete story. Whether Webb's death in 1963 constitutes another in a long list of southern tragedies can only be conjectured.

NOTES

1. Walter Prescott Webb Papers, box 2M248, no. 8, University of Texas Archives, Austin.
2. Ibid.

3. Cf., for instance, J. Frank Dobie, *Southwestern Historical Quarterly* 41 (January 1938): 257–259, and William MacDonald, *New York Times Book Review*, January 9, 1938. The strongest indictment in my memory came from a conversation at Harvard in 1948 (a decade after publication) with Henrietta Larson, the business-history professor and writer.

4. Walter Prescott Webb, "History as High Adventure," in *History as High Adventure*, ed. E. C. Barksdale (Austin: Pemberton Press, 1969), pp. 17–18.

5. Walter Prescott Webb, "The South's Future Prospect," in *The Idea of the South: Pursuit of a Central Theme*, ed. Frank E. Vandiver (Chicago: University of Chicago Press, 1964), p. 69.

6. Ibid., p. 70.

7. Ibid., p. 71.

8. Ibid., pp. 75–78.

9. Ibid., pp. 67–68.

Australians and the Comparative Frontier

W. Turrentine Jackson

In *The Great Frontier*, first published in 1952, Walter Prescott Webb joined the critics who complained that students of the frontier experience in the American West had failed to heed Frederick Jackson Turner's suggestion that comparative studies of frontiers elsewhere in the world were needed. Webb chided historians everywhere when he wrote, "As for historians in other countries, in the New World or the Old World, they have with few exceptions ignored the frontier completely, have never become more than vaguely conscious of its existence."[1] Fortunately for his reputation as a scholar, Webb added a belated footnote, "Canada is an exception. Its proximity to the United States has made it impossible for Canadian historians to escape the frontier hypothesis." With the tremendous array of contemporary publications on the comparative aspects of the Canadian frontier, Webb's timely footnote saved him a bit of embarrassment, if he could be embarrassed by such oversights.[2]

In 1954, the University of Wisconsin sponsored a series of thirteen lectures in a program designated "Wisconsin Reconsiders the Frontier." There Webb presented "The Western World Frontier." He indicated by this time that he was well aware of the international aspects of frontier studies. He observed that the idea of the frontier exercising a profound influence on life, culture, and institutions "is permeating other lands similar to this, such as Canada, Australia, South Africa and New Zealand. It is also being considered by the Latin American countries to the south, and it will in the future be examined elsewhere." If various geographic areas in the Western Hemisphere had been affected by the frontier experience, Webb argued, "this influence was exerted wherever the people of Western Europe took over frontier lands."[3] Rather than examine the parts, Webb had the breadth of vision to see the whole. His message was loud and clear, at least to the editors of *The Frontier in Perspective*, who wrote: "Instead of modifying the Turner hypothesis on the influence of the American frontier, Professor Webb has taken it out of its national encasement and applied it to the world. His hypothesis may well be called the 'Webb thesis.' It poses a distressing question to the modern world: What happens to democracy, capitalism and the other ways of life now that the World Frontier has closed?"[4]

May I suggest that Australians and historians writing about Australia have made a far more significant contribution to our understanding of the comparative aspects of the frontier experience than have their professional colleagues in the United States.[5] Of the three historians outside the United States whom Webb named in *The Great Frontier* as serious students of the frontier, two were Australians: Professor Sir William Keith Hancock, formerly of the University of Melbourne and now at Oxford University, and Fred Alexander of the University of Western Australia.[6]

The descriptive qualities and vivid imagery of Hancock's writing can best be illustrated by a paragraph analogous to Turner's famous Cumberland Gap–South Pass passage relative to the movement of economic types westward as applied to Australia.

There is a famous gap in the range of the Blue Mountains, that wall of rock and scrub which for a quarter of a century hemmed in this colony of New South Wales within the coastal plains. Stand at this gap and watch the frontiers following each other westward—the squatters' frontier which filled the western plains with sheep and laid the foundations of Australia's economy, the miners' frontier which brought Australia population and made her a radical democracy, the farmers' frontier which gradually and painfully tested and proved the controls of Australian soil and climate. Stand a few hundred miles further west on the Darling River and see what these controls have done to the frontier. The farmers have dropped out of the westward-moving procession, beaten by aridity. Only the pastoralists and prospectors pass by. In the west centre of the continent, aridity has beaten even the pastoralists. On the fringe of a dynamic society there are left only a few straggling prospectors and curious anthropologists, infrequent invaders of the aboriginal reserves.[7]

In his brief but influential *Moving Frontiers: An American Theme and Its Application to Australian History*, Fred Alexander considered three topics: Frederick Jackson Turner and the frontier theme, in which he analyzed the relevant critical literature; the effects of the closing of the American frontier; and the frontier theme in Australian history.[8]

While Webb was making the last editorial changes in *The Great Frontier* during the winter of 1951, Norman D. Harper of the University of Melbourne participated in an institute sponsored by the University of Kansas City entitled "The Influence of the West on American Ideas and Institutions" and published his ideas in an article, "Turner the Historian: 'Hypothesis' or 'Process'? With Special Reference to Frontier Society in Australia." Convinced that Turner was primarily concerned with process, Harper examined the successive stages of the frontier's advance in Australia and its effect on democracy, individualism, law and order, political consolidation, and nationalism. He concluded that here, too, was a universal complex process with an "infinite variety of end results" that required comparative study.[9]

Within a month after the appearance of Webb's *The Great Frontier*, Harper published "Frontier and Section: A Turner 'Myth'?" in which he informed his professional colleagues Down Under about the status of the controversy over Turner's ideas in the United States. "Too many historians have rested content with the industrious exploration of 'Turner's Peak' instead of passing through a new Cumberland Gap themselves," he concluded; he also suggested, "Turner admitted his ignorance of the Canadian process, and might have added Siberia and Latin America to his list. Comparative study and the application of Turnerian and later techniques to new fields [are] now in progress and a modified frontier hypothesis may ultimately emerge as a formal thesis."[10]

Webb's *Great Frontier* may well have been a contributing factor to the upsurge of interest in the study of the frontier experience and in a reconsideration of Turner's hypothesis and methodology as applied to other nations. Paul F. Sharp wrote "Three Frontiers: Some Comparative Studies of Canadian, American, and Australian Settlement," suggesting a more systematic approach to comparative analysis. Three conditions appeared essential to meaningful comparisons: settlement had to occur in approximately the same span of time; the cultural and technological heritages needed to be similar; and the physical environments needed to be somewhat alike. Although Sharp doubted that any new sweeping interpretation of the impact of frontiers on western civilization would emerge, he was convinced that comparative studies would broaden our understanding of the influence of frontier experiences and test the validity of past interpretations.[11] At the Madison meeting, A. L. Burt, long a student of the Canadian frontier, addressed himself to the question in his talk "If Turner Had Looked at Canada, Australia, and New Zealand When He Wrote about the West" and explored, among other ideas, the impact of squatters, miners, and farmers on the land policy and evolution of government in Australia.[12]

Among British historians, Harry C. Allen was foremost in the study of the American frontier. In his essay "F. J. Turner and the Frontier in American History," contributed to *British Essays in American History*, Allen recognized the importance of Webb's contribution when he wrote: "We are now in a position to restore that sense of perspective and to see the American experience as part of the experience of mankind. The frontier of the United States was one among many; it was but a part, as W. P. Webb has pointed out, of 'the great frontier' of Western civilization. The expansion of the United States was merely one aspect of the huge expansion of the European peoples into the sparsely settled areas of the globe, which took place between the fifteenth and the twentieth centuries."[13] Allen turned his attention to a comparison of the frontier in Australia and the United States in *Bush and Backwoods* and resolved, first, "to consider for a brief moment the relationship of the two histories in time; next, to compare the environments and the peoples environed; then to contrast the way those people made their living; and after that to attempt a comparison of the effects of the frontier environment upon them. In the end, it may be possible to cast a gleam of light upon the validity of the frontier thesis."[14]

Australian Russel Ward explored the impact of the frontier upon Australian attitudes in his delightful book, *The Australian Legend*. Using old "anonymous" bush songs as historical evidence in the development of a national mystique, Ward concluded that an Australian way of looking at people and events grew up first among the bush workers in the Australian pastoral industry. He argued that this group had a disproportionate influence on the attitude of the entire Australian nation. In a summary chapter, "Two Noble Frontiersmen," he made some incisive observations concerning the difference in the impact of the frontier on Australia and the United States. For example, he indicated that in Australia the frontier did not have as great a lasting effect on "the external forms of life" as in the United States. The Australian frontier had a much greater effect upon people's attitude toward life and, therefore, upon the way in which political and legal institutions were made to work in practice. The change in intellectual outlook was more important than the change in political structure.[15]

What have these historians, and many others not mentioned, taught us about the frontier experience in Australia?[16] Some have contemplated the procession of frontiersmen, or rather the stages of development along the lines suggested by Turner. Perhaps first mention should be made of the convict frontier. Analogies abound. The prisoners supplied a cheap supply of labor comparable to indentured servants in America, while conditions on convict transports were not unlike those on slave ships. Gang labor and the use of chains and the lash characterized both the cotton plantation and the pastoral lease. The British government sanctioned and British capitalists financed and exploited both slavery and the convict system.[17]

During the second stage of advance, explorers discovered passes through the Blue Mountains and thereby opened up the grasslands beyond. One immediately is reminded of Daniel Boone crossing the Cumberland Gap to settle the pasture lands of Kentucky and Tennessee. Restless sheepmen hemmed in between the Blue Mountains and the sea followed the tracks left by explorers to begin a third stage of advance, the squatters' frontier. The government of New South Wales, unable to control the occupation of interior lands, tried in 1829 to limit settlement to the established counties. The analogy with the Proclamation Line of 1763 in the American colonies is obvious. Neither succeeded in checking the western march. The advance of this squatters' frontier occurred not along any single, unbroken line. Sheepmen drove herds into western New South Wales, present Victoria, and further inland from coastal areas near the colonies at Adelaide, Perth, and Moreton Bay and Cape York in Queensland. Before the end of the great squatting age, 1830–1847, the entire southeast of the continent was filled with sheep.[18]

The frontier pattern shifted steadily with the discovery of gold at Bathurst, Bendigo, and Ballarat in 1851.[19] The pattern of gold rushes, in general, was similar world-wide.[20] Nevertheless, there were several basic differences between the experiences of Australia and Western America. In the United States there was only one land law, that of the federal government; in Australia, land law and policy varied from colony to colony. Free to roam about, miners became squatters on the public domain in the United States prior to 1866; in Australia the government supervised the rushes by granting miners' licenses and appointing autocratic gold commissioners, who inspected these licenses, determined who had the right to dig, and established the size of claims in the district.[21] Australians boast that law and order prevailed on the mining frontier. The only significant outbreak of violence, at the Eureka stockade, the closest the country ever came to revolution, resulted from governmental suppression and neglect, real or imagined.[22]

Perhaps more important, Australian mining discoveries were not in isolated regions but within the area of pastoral settlement and in the cases of Ballarat and Bendigo in close proximity to Melbourne. The question has been asked, "Did the miners stay long enough to have a permanent impact?"[23]

Finally, with the decline of the mining frontier, there developed what might be termed the selectors' frontier. Miners joined forces with farmers in an attempt to "unlock the lands" and open up the large squatting runs of the pastoralists for agricultural settlement. This crusade ended in failure.

Historians have suggested that the attempt to organize a discussion of the frontier experience in the United States as a steady and orderly western procession of people on the basis of their economic pursuits tends to distort the evidence, no matter how helpful it may be to textbook writers in providing them with a table of contents. The same can be said of Australia. Perhaps a more fruitful approach would be to look at comparative frontiers as underdeveloped regions with a high ratio of land to people in which the penetration of these regions to utilize natural resources influenced native inhabitants as well as newcomers and changed their material well-being, institutions, social status, and intellectual outlook. In this process of modifying the environment, encouraging population growth, improving transportation, and mobilizing and marketing production, two interrelated, dominant forces encouraged, modified, and shaped the efforts of individuals—political governments and investment capital.

Physical geography and environmental conditions had a significant impact on Australia's frontier. The plains inland from the eastern and southeastern coastal fringe covered an area that was only a fraction of the size of the fertile lands in the United States between the Alleghenies and the eastern border of the Great Plains. The dry heart of Australia has been compared to the Great Plains, once called the "Great American Desert." In some ways the historical significance of the ninety-eighth meridian, which figured so prominently in Webb's *The Great Plains*, and of Goyder's line of "safe settlement" in South Australia is remarkably similar. In both cases those who crossed the line faced institutional and cultural adjustments. Changes in land-use patterns, the application of technological improvements, and the introduction of new crops, however, did not increase productivity in Australia as in the United States. Much of the Australian Outback, particularly the Red Desert Center, remains less habitable than the Colorado and Mojave deserts of the American Southwest. Indeed, it has been suggested that Australia never had a frontier, only the Outback. There are two unequal parts to the continent: *economic* Australia and *empty* Australia. In addition to aridity, Australia is characterized by a warm climate, an absence of mountains any higher than the Appalachians, and inadequate water, except for underground sources tapped by artesian wells in some areas. Its soils are poor, its forests meager. Most important is the inadequacy of the rivers. A few short streams run to the sea from the eastern coastal range or in the far north, but there is only one continental river, the Murray, that drains an area about 40 percent of the size of that drained by the Mississippi. Under these circumstances, the struggle against nature has proved a major factor in the frontier experience in Australia. The American pioneers found a much more hospitable environment and their efforts were far more economically rewarding.[24]

There has always been a notable contrast in the immigration patterns in Australia and the United States. Far more homogeneous, Australia contains 97 percent British stock and as high as 99 percent "unmixed" European stock. The "White Australia Policy" began with the rejection of British proposals that loyalists during the American Revolution emigrate with their Negro slaves and that Pacific island women be imported for the male convicts. During the frontier period, Australia sacrificed much of the cultural diversity contributed by various racial groups and nationalities found in America in order to achieve greater economic opportunity and political unity. The "New Australians" of the twentieth century, chiefly Italians and Greeks, have only partially redressed this balance. In both Australia and the United States, Chinese came to work in the gold fields and in both instances they faced hostility and eventual exclusion.

Contacts between the whites and the natives in Australia witnessed no strong aboriginal resistance comparable to that of the Indians on the frontiers of the United States. Natives had divided Australia into tribal areas with well-defined and recognized boundaries that none dared to trespass. According to aboriginal legends, tribal ancestors had traveled through these specified lands establishing sacred places. A strong bond developed within each tribe due to the belief that both their spirits and those of their ancestors would continue to occupy this territory until they were incarnated. Aboriginal retreat meant not only loss of land with the natural resources for survival but also destruction of the aborigines' spiritual past, present, and hopes for the future. To resist meant slaughter and to migrate meant warfare with other tribesmen. In despair, the natives often refrained from having children or destroyed them at birth.[25]

In spite of degradation or destruction, aboriginal resistance was never strong enough to require a series of colonial conferences to plan a united program of defense or aggression.[26] There were no frontier military posts to become schools of local self-government, as described by Turner on the American frontier.[27] British humanitarian and missionary interests counseled moderation in both countries but had little success in checking exploitation and violence. Comparatively speaking, the historian must conclude that the record of destruction and neglect of the Australian aboriginal is far worse than that of the American Indian.[28] The Canadian experience stands in remarkable contrast to both. Because law arrived in the virtually uninhabited Canadian West before the settlers, the Indians could adjust gradually to the cultural changes associated with sedentary life. Incorruptible agents, who treated the natives with respect and honesty, assisted in this transition.

Nothing interested the frontiersman more than the availability of land and the government's policy in granting it. In Australia the Crown owned all lands and during the first forty-three years of settlement it transferred land by grants in fee simple. Little land was sold prior to 1831, but in that year the government established a minimum price of five shillings an acre in hopes of providing income to subsidize emigration and thus increase a desperately needed supply of labor. In 1838, the price of land increased to twelve shillings, or three dollars, an acre, primarily to keep the labor force on the job and to thwart economic independence.

This determination of the British imperial government to keep land prices high ran counter to that of pastoralists to gain control of acreage on the fringes of settlement. Consequently, a series of acts was passed as a compromise to permit squatting, under restrictions, not unlike the principle of preemption in the United States. In 1842, the price of land rose to twenty shillings, or five dollars, an acre outside the original nineteen counties of New South Wales, and there it remained for twenty years. However, five thousand free persons with three thousand assigned servants had already occupied over seven hundred stations, or ranches, as squatters. Simultaneously, New South

Wales obtained self-government through a representative council. This body immediately granted security of tenure to squatters through a preemptive right to occupy their holdings from one to fourteen years on the basis of the density of settlement. It authorized "independent" appraisals to fix lease charges and prohibited trespassing. When a British Order-in-Council endorsed these colonial regulations in 1847, the squatting interests were entrenched.[29]

With mining discoveries, the first gold commissioners in New South Wales and Victoria, ignorant of California practices, assigned claims to those possessing a license anywhere from one-tenth to one-twentieth the size of the California norm. This action vastly increased the number of miners and encouraged fierce competition and deprivation. Alluvial, or placer, claims were as small as eight feet by eight feet until the government introduced a policy of twelve feet square in April 1853. Claims in most California mining districts were twenty-five times as large as those in New South Wales and seventy times those in Victoria.[30] The Crown retained mineral rights when grants of land were sold. Miners operated by obtaining a right, not unlike a lease, or a use permit. Where minerals had passed into private ownership, men holding miners' rights could enter private property and remove minerals by paying a royalty to the private owner. The initial mining rushes proved transitory and did little to open the country's natural resources at a time when a few pastoral squatters dominated. The unsuccessful digger was driven from the gold fields back to his previous or a new occupation or to the site of a new mineral discovery.

Just as the center of mining activity moved from California to Nevada and Colorado, on to Idaho and Montana and elsewhere in the United States, so "the rush that never ended" in Australia moved on to Charters Towers and Mount Morgan in Queensland and to Coolgardie and Kalgoorlie in Western Australia.[31] There was a continuous exchange of information between engineers in the United States and Australia, and application of scientific and technical knowledge to the processes of mining and smelting ore revived the economy of entire districts. The impact of this knowledge as applied at Black Hawk in Colorado, at the Homestake mine in South Dakota, or at Bingham in Utah was no greater than at Broken Hill in western New South Wales, at Mount Isa in Queensland, or at Mount Lyell in Tasmania.[32] The role of foreign investment, chiefly British, in the development of mineral resources in the two countries will provide valuable insights of a comparative nature.[33]

Following the initial impact of gold discoveries on the Australian economy, a campaign was launched to make the country's lands more widely available for agricultural purposes. The Australian land system had favored large pastoralists at the expense of small settlers, largely because of the ever-increasing demand of Yorkshire textile-mill owners for wool clip. Meanwhile, Australia's first mining frontiers had led to a significant increase in population demanding food. Miners who had struck it rich wanted to invest in property, and some unsuccessful diggers wanted, if possible, to get back to the land. So miners joined forces with farmers in an attempt to unlock the lands, by opening up the leased squatting runs of pastoralists for agricultural settlement. The passage of Robertson's Free Selection Act in New South Wales in 1861 proved a major departure in land policy. Anyone—man, woman, or child—could obtain a tract of land from 40 to 640 acres from the unoccupied Crown lands, prior to survey, for payment at the going price of twenty shillings, or one pound, an acre, payable in equal installments over a four-year period. An initial deposit of ten dollars was required, along with residency and improvement provisions.

Squatters organized to defeat both the purpose and the spirit of this law in ways similar to the violation of the Homestead Act in the United States. With financial backing from banks or pastoral companies that handled their wool, they took advantage of the law's provision allowing everyone over two years of age to file a claim. Relatives, friends, dependents, and even paupers in retirement homes made applications by the thousands. Shrewd blackmailers and dummy entrymen filed claims on the limited number of water holes on the sheep runs, a common practice known as "peacocking," or picking the eyes out of the peacock. In Victoria the Crown opened up the lands to selectors in three stages between 1861 and 1865 on terms similar to those in New South Wales, but selection occurred *after*, not before, survey. Squatters proved so skillful in holding the most fertile lands that the selectors', or farmers', frontier had to jump across the pastoralists into the drier regions of the mallee.

In South Australia the frontier moved too rapidly and wheat farmers often experienced defeat in trying to conquer the environment. As noted earlier, the Australian pattern of occupation and attempts to solve the problems of aridity paralleled experience on the Great Plains of the United States. Geography, climate, and the machinations of squatters combined to delay profitable, small-scale agriculture until the 1890s, and by then the pastoralists controlled most of the good arable lands.

Thus, efforts to democratize landholding failed. At the same time many large graziers had overextended themselves by borrowing to expand their acreage and flocks, and their vast domains became the property of the great pastoral companies. Control by financiers replaced that of the producers. The result was the establishment of what Brian Fitzpatrick has described in "The Big Man's Frontier."[34] Perhaps the most significant difference in the American and Australian frontiers was the much smaller amount of freehold land obtained by individual frontiersmen in Australia. Moreover, the Australian pastoral industry differed from the range cattle and sheep industries of the American West, for matters of international trade and marketing, urban finance, and estate management played a much larger and much earlier role in Australia.

The theme of the interrelationship between private enterprise and government in developing the natural resources and the economy of Australia was most apparent in the areas of water, timber, and railroads. Pastoralists made an attempt to augment their limited water supply by sinking expensive artesian bores in scattered geological basins, especially in Queensland. There they dammed the supply at the site and transported it through earthen channels where needed. Unfit for human consumption, the water could be used for stock and improvement of grasslands. In the 1880s the Chaffey brothers brought modern irrigation to Australia and developed the centers of settlement at Mildura in Victoria and Renmark in South Australia. Although suffering technical and financial reverses, they laid the foundations for future government aid to irrigation districts.[35] A notable example of state support was the water scheme of western Australia to supply the gold fields at Coolgardie and Kalgoorlie. Five million gallons of water a day were pumped from the coast through a thirty-inch pipe for 351 miles eastward into the desert, aiding in the development of agricultural areas to the north and south of the main pipeline.[36]

When the national government tried to transfer control of the waters of navigable streams to the Commonwealth, Victoria and New South Wales objected, insisting upon the right of states to the reasonable use of water for irrigation and conservation. Between 1913 and 1917, however, the prime minister and the premiers of the states concerned worked out the terms of the Murray River Agreement, obtained legislative approval, and established a permanent commission to administer a program for the conservation of Murray waters.[37] United States historians are immediately reminded of the Colorado River Agreement. In both countries responsibility for water conservation and irrigation passed from private hands to colony or state and finally to a national government.

The history of the western Australian timber industry, with its five million acres of majestic jarrah and karri trees, provides another example of the exploitation and conservation of a basic resource. Initially unregulated, the industry was developed by eastern capitalists with narrow-gauge railways, steam engines to haul felled trees by chains to the railways, and mills to process timber. They sold out to English capitalists, who, by 1898, had organized nine companies with more than two million pounds invested. In 1919, the Forests Department was established, placing four-fifths of the acreage under the supervision of the state with only those holding licenses permitted to cut. In a superb example of how to manage a natural resource to prevent exhaustion, government foresters marked trees to be felled and rangers supervised both cutting and reforestation.[38]

Although private enterprise initially constructed Australian railroads, first efforts led to financial disaster and bankruptcy. To attract capital from investors who found greater profits elsewhere, several colonies provided financial assistance and land grants for railroad construction.[39] When this aid proved inadequate, colonial governments undertook railroad construction and borrowed heavily, chiefly in Britain, to provide essential capital. Invariably, these railway systems became radial networks, built with a different gauge in each state. They offered preferential freight rates to make certain that commerce went to each capital city.[40] Only after establishment of the Commonwealth was it possible to work toward an integrated national system of railroads, to standardize gauges, and to undertake construction of the east-west transcontinental railroad. Meanwhile, numerous narrow-gauge lines had opened up extensive areas for development of natural resources where more expensive and heavier standard-gauge roads would have been uneconomical and difficult to construct. One cannot escape the conclusion, however, that the government played a much larger role in making natural resources accessible and marketable in Australia than in the United States.

Emphasis on the economic development of the frontier's natural resources should not cause us to overlook comparative social changes. Focusing briefly on the impact of the frontier experience on the life style of people in Australia and America, the comparisons and parallels appear endless. Housing in the Outback—consisting of canvas stretched on poles, a bush lean-to, or a log or split-slab hut with chimney of stone and mud—was similar to that found in the mining camps or homesteads in the American West. In wooded areas frontiersmen cleared the land by "ring barking" in Australia, "girdling" in America. The ox was the beast of burden in Australia, where the "bullocky" with his dray was the counterpart of the bullwhacker with his freight wagon. Pioneer transportation was by "bus coaches" of Cobb and Company, whose activities were comparable to those of Wells, Fargo and Company. The railroads replaced stagecoaches earlier in the United States, for they were still being used in Queensland as late as 1924. Experiments with camels, tried in both countries, were more extensive and lasted longer in the desert heartland of Australia. In the cattle country the man on horseback, whether he be cowboy or jackaroo, contributed to the cult of masculinity. Settlers used barbed wire for fencing in both instances, and the business of branding, castrating, and selecting cattle for the market was similar though termed a "muster" in Australia rather than a "roundup." As farmers moved into inhospitable land, the job of removing thickets of mallee was as backbreaking as plowing up the prairie sod. In the subhumid areas the introduction of dry-farming techniques, artesian wells, and windmills and the adaptation of machinery provided by innovative technology made survival possible.[41]

What were the effects of the frontier experience in Australia? Was the frontier the area of the most rapid and effective nationalization as Turner suggested it was for America? The verdict appears to be "no," largely because the frontier had a comparatively limited period of influence. Urbanization was well advanced by the time of the gold rushes, and it increased thereafter. As in the United States, immigrants tended to congregate in the great coastal cities. Even so, Russel Ward has reminded us that in both countries there has been "an unconscious search for a folk-hero who could symbolize the nation" and suggests there was no more likely candidate than the frontiersman. He notes that the *average* American or Australian is not the same as the *typical* American or Australian and hints that Australians "at the edge of settlement did rather more than their share to make our country what it is."[42]

What effect did the frontier have upon the growth of Australian democracy, in all the ways Turner used that term in describing the American experience? Concerning political democracy, Professor Alexander concluded that Australian democracy owed much of its direction and influence to the mining frontiers of the 1850s. In contrast, Professor Harper believed that the pastoralists suppressed the economic goals of the miners and the farmer through political action and insisted that "Australian democracy clearly did not come out of the miner's shanty or the squatter's study."[43] Professor Allen reminds us that, although miners did make their influence felt, the battle for self-government in the colonies was largely won before the gold rushes.[44] In balance, Alexander showed insight many years ago when he suggested that the "posthumous influence" of the frontier in Australian democracy was "small by comparison with the influence it still exercises in the United States."[45]

On other facets of democracy—opportunity and individualism—Australia offers some startling contrasts to the American experience. Turner repeatedly suggested that individualism based upon the opportunity to obtain free land was the most important component of American frontier democracy. The typical frontiersman in Australia was not an individualist farmer tilling his own soil with the help of his family and perhaps a few hired hands. Instead he was a wage earner who usually did not expect to improve his status. Russel Ward has noted that the frontiersman's isolation in the Outback taught him cooperation, as on the American frontier, but his economic interests, unlike the American's, reinforced his tendency to support a social, or collectivist, viewpoint.[46]

At one time, Australians had both geographic and social mobility as well as New World egalitarian ideas opposed to privilege. Optimistic in outlook and preoccupied with the pursuit of material things, they probably had a higher standard of living than in the United States in the mid–nineteenth century. However, the catastrophic economic reverses of the 1890s forced the Australian to lean upon the state for support.[47] The frontier and, especially, urban areas supported the collectivism that emphasized the protection of the wage earner and championed the cause of the underdog. The solidarity of the workingman was symbolized in the Australian doctrine of "matesmanship," a sentiment of cardinal importance in the country's ethos. Shrinking opportunity made enforced equality an Australian passion, even a fetish. Allen aptly expressed the contrast when he wrote, "Australia desires to keep all her sons at the same economic level, America to make hers behave alike."[48] Life in the Australian bush was too harsh and degrading to have an appeal comparable to that of the farmer on the American frontier. In one instance hard work led to individual ownership of land, and in the other to remaining a wage earner. This fact more than any other resulted in the United States's being a middle-class nation dedicated to capital enterprise, while Australia became a working-class community emphasizing a more extensive welfare state.[49]

Some of the adjectives that Turner used to describe the frontier's contribution to American character may well apply as aptly to the Australian: coarseness and strength, acuteness and inquisitiveness, buoyancy and exuberance. Yet, when one considers materialism, an element of doubt creeps in, particularly in reflecting on the contemporary heritage of the frontier. Denied an opportunity for material success by limited natural resources and a hostile climate, the Australian refuses to place the same importance on worldly goods as does the American. He rejects the perfectionism cherished as part of American life, particularly the dependence upon mechanical objects or gadgets. The Australian prides himself on making do with what he has and ventures forth with an attitude that finds expression in two well-known phrases, "she'll be right, mate," and "give it a go."

Although Australians boast of the comparative lack of physical violence and disorder on the frontier, they know that frontiersmen had a mistrust, even contempt, for the law and a basic dislike of authority. "Waltzing Matilda," the most popular of the Australian folk songs, epitomizes this attitude. According to Norman Harper:

The real hero of Waltzing Matilda *is neither the "squatter mounted on his thoroughbred" nor the "troopers, one, two, three" who were assisting him to recover the straying "jumbuck." It is rather the "swagman" who "shoved the jumbuck into his tucker bag" and who suicided into the billabong rather than accept arrest for stealing sheep. During the great squatting age it was the bushranger who so frequently became the hero. . . . above all Ned Kelly. The brutal murders of the Kelly gang have been forgotten in the legend of heroic resistance to authority, in the admiration of Ned Kelly's last stand in his home made armour before he was brought down by the troopers firing at his unprotected legs. "Game as Ned Kelly" represents high praise from an Australian.*[50]

Every Australian is proud of Ned Kelly, "the jolly swagman" known as the Wild Colonial Boy. The American outlaw has never been the hero that the Australian bushranger has been. Much of the glamor of the American cowboy has been attached to the bushranger. An explanation of how this has come about is not easy. One historian has suggested that it results from a "curious confusion of pity for the criminal with contempt for the law" derived in part from the nation's history of authoritarianism, its convict origins, and its reaction to an environment that permitted only a few to achieve success.[51] Another has explained the phenomenon by the maladjustment of the law and institutions at a time of social and economic change, particularly antiquated land regulations enacted to meet the needs of another day.[52] The immediate results of all this can be seen in a basic dislike, even hatred, of the police by Australians to the present day.

It should also be noted that one does not find in Australia the restlessness, the nervous energy, and the furious pace of life that characterize the United States. Harry Allen has suggested that Australians expend their last ounce of energy reluctantly for fear that when disaster strikes they may not have the reserves of strength to meet the crisis. "Go-getting" is not considered a virtue in the mind of the Australian.[53]

Perhaps Russel Ward has written the most thoughtful summary on the frontier experience in Australia and the United States:

There is every reason to think that the frontier tradition has been, at least, not less influential and persistent in Australia than America. But the really interesting puzzle is why, in the nineteenth century and particularly toward the end of it, the frontier should have possessed so much prestige. Why should so many men have paid to the relatively uncouth frontiersman the supreme compliment of imitating, often unconsciously, his manners and outlook? . . .

In the broadest possible terms it may be suggested that admiration for the "simple" virtues of the barbarian or the frontiersman is a sentiment which arises naturally in highly complex, megalopolitan societies.[54]

More recently, the contemporary difference in Australian and American characteristics has been explained in the contrasting power of private business and economic prosperity, with the following result:

Where Americans have glorified individual success, Australians have developed a mythology of mateship. Where Americans have become notorious for their pace of living, their emphasis upon success and their endless endeavours at "getting ahead," Australians have tended to favour leisure, to emphasize "creature comforts" and to be satisfied with "getting-by." Where Americans have stressed a serious and industrious attitude toward work, Australians have approved a more easy-going attitude expressed in the idioms "near enough" or "she'll be right." Where Americans have characteristically moralized about the role of good character and hard work to the attainment of success, Australians have been rather more realistic about the role of luck. Where Americans have stressed the self-help doctrine of "rugged individualism," Australians have demanded a "fair go," which frequently meant government assistance. Where American reformers have concentrated their attention upon keeping the race for success open, Australians have shunned the notion of a race and focused upon some of the social requirements of those in need. And where the American version of equality means opportunity to traverse the many levels of the success ladder, thus producing inequalities, the Australian version includes a much greater measure of levelling in its desire for "equality of enjoyment."[55]

Just as the 1930s inaugurated two decades of criticism and revisionism of Turner's ideas and methodology in the United States, the last two decades have seen Australian historians minimize the importance of the bush. Paul Sharp warned impatiently that "to explain Canadian and Australian democracy, nationalism, or culture in terms of frontier influences alone can meet with no more success than to interpret American life solely in such terms."[56] He suggested many areas for comparative analysis that might prove more fruitful. Historians are currently exploring the theoretical and methodological ways whereby these comparisons can best be made.[57]

Norman Harper has also noted that the frontier experience has received far greater attention by United States historians than by Australians.[58] The statement is correct, but much more than American scholars, all those writing about the Australian frontier have kept comparative analysis constantly in view. Professor Allen concluded that the Australian comparison provided a greater understanding of the Turner thesis, and he came away from his study and sojourn in Australia as one of the most ardent supporters of Turner's ideas in the Anglo-American world.[59] Although he saw more similarity between Australianization and Americanization, the promotion of democracy, and the exploitation of the natural resources than warranted, he has noted many striking contrasts in the history of the two countries that have caused other historians to seek explanations elsewhere.

A marked departure in the study of Australian character and the growth of nationality occurred with the publication in 1957 of George Nadel's *Australia's Colonial Culture: Ideals, Men, and Institutions in Mid–Nineteenth Century Eastern Australia*. Nadel discussed the cultural baggage that individuals brought from an old land to a new and how knowledge and ideas were diffused in the search for social harmony, cohesion, and unity. Specifically, he probed the mind of the immigrant and the changes in his thinking brought about by the press, libraries, and discussions of popular education and attitudes toward religion. The towns naturally received far more attention than the bush. Nadel regretted the preoccupation with economic interpretation on the part of Australian scholars. Moreover, he suggested that the Australian's view of nationality was found, not within the political framework, but in ethical and human concerns. "The curious fact that Australia's only genuine folk hero is not a statesman or patriot, but a bushranger executed in 1880," he suggested, "is significant of the depth of the appreciation of the human quality in relation to national memory." There is not even a courteous nod in the direction of the frontier, geographic environmentalism, or economic determinism in this intellectual history, other than to dismiss it as the "important myth" of the bush.[60]

Ten years lapsed before Australian historians suddenly produced three books on the history of ideas.[61] Immediately, a renewed interest appeared in the moral and intellectual foundations of the nation among academics, with the usual plea for more investigation.[62]

The intellectual and cultural historians interested in less emphasis on the frontier were joined by those pleading for more attention to urban developments in hopes of restoring a balance to Australian historical investigation. In his "The Study of Australian History, 1929–1959," Professor J. A. LaNauze, as president of the Australian Association for the Advancement of Science, lamented, "the early existence of relatively large-scale urban life on this continent of small total population, has failed to impress Australian historians."[63] Norman Harper and others have also been concerned that Australian historians in general have lagged at least a generation behind their American colleagues, and they might add Canadian as well, in the study of the city: "The urban frontier is almost virgin territory."[64] This neglect on the part of the scholarly community is surprising when one recognizes the urban heritage of Australia. In 1850, over 20 percent of Australians lived in towns compared to 15 percent in the United States. By 1921, 63 percent of Australians were city dwellers compared to 51 percent in America. By 1950, the comparison remained 69 to 59 percent, still in favor of the Australians.

Australian historians studying the frontier should not be singled out for criticism for their lack of concern with urban studies, because they have continued to note both the importance and the neglect of the subject by their colleagues. As early as 1940, Fred Alexander wrote, "it is time to call a halt to appraising frontier influence on Australian democracy and to look instead for the influence of urban industrialization which in Australia preceded as well as accompanied the closing of the frontier."[65] Harry Allen also demonstrated that Australia has been more highly urbanized than the United States and suggested, "As a higher and higher proportion of Australians, immigrants as well as those born in the antipodes, came to reside in the great coastal cities, these became the chief areas of Australianization."[66]

Australian economic historians and those trained in economics have paid tribute to the city. In 1958, N. G. Butlin laid down as one of twelve cardinal principles for a reappraisal of Australian economic history that "Australian economic development is mainly a story of urbanization. The building of cities absorbed the greater part of Australian resources diverted to development purposes; the operation of enterprises in towns employed most of the increasing population engaged in work."[67] In his subsequent studies on the effect of foreign investment and borrowing on Australian domestic production and economic development, he carefully documented the dominant role of urban institutions. A. R. Hall has explored the same theme of the role of British investors in Australia, and his account of the Stock Exchange of Melbourne illustrates the impact of that city upon the economic growth of Victoria. J. D. Bailey's recent monograph on the pastoral industry emphasizes the key importance of company banking and financial policy for over a century.[68]

In 1959 Brisbane became the first of the great capital cities seriously studied by historians, and the investigation of that urban complex has continued.[69] Alan Birch and David S. Macmillan, in *The Sydney Scene, 1788–1960*, view that city from many vantage points through the assembled accounts of many observers.[70] Geoffrey Serle has described the role of "Marvelous Melbourne" in *The Rush to Be Rich*.[71] Social and cultural historians are closing ranks with the economic historians in Australia in a mutual concern with the urban past. Ronald Lawson, an urban historian, has recently asserted, in fact, that "the core of Ward's thesis—that the so-called 'bush ethos' was accepted by urban Australia during the 1890's—is wrong. . . . It seems likely that the sense of egalitarianism, such as it was, will be found to be rooted as deeply in the apparently fluid social structure of the cities, where no great gulf separated class from class, as in the matesmanship of the bush workers."[72]

One can do no less than to wish the metropolitan and intellectual historians well, to "give it a go," and at the same time to express the hope that they will not be disappointed when the Australian public, as well as the inhabitants of the "Great Frontier," fails to recognize their achievement. As in the United States, where the citizen interested in history delights in accounts of buffaloes, coyotes, and jack rabbits, of Indians, bullwhackers, Pony Express riders, and stage drivers, of prospectors and prostitutes, and, above all, of the lawman and the cowboy, so in Australia he is likely to direct his attention to kangaroos, dingoes, emus, and koalas, to aborigines, to the bullocky, to diggers and jackaroos, and, most important, to the bushranger. Myths have a way of surviving after facts are forgotten.

NOTES

1. Walter Prescott Webb, *The Great Frontier* (Austin: University of Texas Press, 1964), p. 6.
2. Throughout his career Professor Webb was far more interested in developing and writing about his own ideas than in appraising the views of others. He studiously avoided academic debate when possible, preferred to write for periodicals reaching a larger audience than did academic journals, and often boasted to me about his prowess in avoiding book reviewing for professional publications. His pride in being a maverick is well expressed in his presidential address to the American Historical Association, "History as High Adventure," *American Historical Review* 64 (January 1959): 265–281, and in his *An Honest Preface and Other Essays* (Boston: Houghton Mifflin Co., 1959; ed. Joe B. Frantz).
3. Walker D. Wyman and Clifton B. Kroeber, eds., *The Frontier in Perspective* (Madison: University of Wisconsin Press, 1957), pp. 59–77.
4. Ibid., p. 111.
5. The decision to direct my attention to previous scholarship relative to the Australian frontier is an outgrowth of an opportunity to study in that country under the auspices of the American Council of Learned Societies.
6. Webb, *The Great Frontier*, pp. 6–7.
7. William Keith Hancock, *Survey of British Commonwealth Affairs*, vol. 2, *Problems of Economic Policy, 1918–1939* (London: Oxford University Press, 1940), part 50, pp. 2–3. This passage is one most often quoted in Australian historical literature. I found it as irresistible as did Fred Alexander in *Moving Frontiers: An American*

Theme and Its Application to Australian History (Melbourne: Melbourne University Press, 1947), pp. 29–30; Norman D. Harper, "Turner the Historian: 'Hypothesis' or 'Process'? With Special Reference to Frontier Society in Australia," *University of Kansas City Review* 18 (Autumn 1951): 77–78; Paul F. Sharp, "Three Frontiers: Some Comparative Studies of Canadian, American, and Australian Settlement," *Pacific Historical Review* 24 (November 1955): 371–372; Marvin W. Mikesell, "Comparative Studies in Frontier History," *Annals of the Association of American Geographers* 50 (March 1960): 70; and many others. For a comment on Sir William Keith Hancock's writing, see Keith Sinclair, "On Writing Shist," *Historical Studies* 13 (October 1968): 426–432.

8. Alexander, *Moving Frontiers.*

9. Harper, "Turner the Historian."

10. Norman D. Harper, "Frontier and Section: A Turner 'Myth'?" *Historical Studies: Australia and New Zealand* 5 (May 1952): 135–153.

11. Sharp, "Three Frontiers," pp. 369–377.

12. Wyman and Kroeber, eds., *The Frontier in Perspective*, pp. 112–113.

13. Harry C. Allen and C. P. Hill, eds., *British Essays in American History* (New York: St. Martin's Press, 1957), pp. 145–166.

14. Harry C. Allen, *Bush and Backwoods: A Comparison of the Frontier in Australia and the United States* (East Lansing: Michigan State University Press, 1959), pp. v–xv.

15. Russel Ward, *The Australian Legend* (Melbourne: Oxford University Press, 1958), pp. v, 222.

16. I crave the indulgence of both my readers and the historians whose studies I have utilized in preparing this essay for the extensive quotations and close paraphrasing of many of their ideas. Scholars concerned with frontier influences in the American West are acutely sensitive to semantics, and I have cautiously tried not to misrepresent the views of others, as many have done in the case of Frederick Jackson Turner. My purpose in writing this historiographical essay is to bring to the attention of United States historians, even to many specializing in the American West, a body of historical literature that is largely unknown to them.

17. Allen, *Bush and Backwoods*, pp. 18–21, 39–40.

18. The concept of stages of the frontier in Australia is described more fully in Harper, "Turner the Historian." For a full discussion of squatting, see Stephen H. Roberts, *The Squatting Age in Australia, 1835–1847* (Melbourne: Melbourne University Press, 1935 and 1964). A shorter summation is available in Roberts, *History of Land Settlement, 1788–1920* (Melbourne: Melbourne University Press, 1924; New York: Johnson Reprint Corporation, 1968), parts 1–3, and Allen, *Bush and Backwoods*, pp. 55–57. A recent scholarly monograph is D. B. Waterson, *Squatter, Selector, and Storekeeper: A History of Darling Downs, 1859–1893* (Sydney: Sydney University Press, 1968). For the viewpoint of the geographer, see the excellent monograph by T. M. Perry, *Australia's First Frontier: The Spread of Settlement in New South Wales, 1788–1829* (Melbourne: Melbourne University Press, 1963).

19. Geoffrey Serle, *The Golden Age: A History of the Colony of Victoria, 1851–1861* (Melbourne: Melbourne University Press, 1963), pp. 9–36.

20. All students interested in comparative aspects of gold rushes should begin with reading W. P. Morrell, *The Gold Rushes* (New York: Macmillan Co., 1941).

21. Lewis Lloyd, "The Sources and Development of Australian Mining Law," Doctoral dissertation, Australian National University, 1966. This is a thorough discussion from the lawyer's viewpoint. Appendix 3, "The Development of U.S. Mining Law: A Comparative Survey," is most helpful.

22. Bruce Kent, "Agitations on the Victorian Gold Fields, 1851–1854," *Historical Studies: Australia and New Zealand* 6 (November 1954): 261–281. In a recent study of the involvement of Americans in the disturbances on the Victorian gold fields, Daniel and Annette Potts conclude that, although Americans hoped that Australia would become a democratic republic, they were determined that it should be achieved by orderly and legal means (see E. Daniel and Annette Potts, "American Republicanism and Disturbances on the Victorian Goldfields," *Historical Studies* 13 [April 1968]: 145–164). For a full treatment of Americans and the gold rush of the 1850s, see their *Young America and Australian Gold* (Brisbane: University of Queensland Press, 1974).

23. Alexander, *Moving Frontiers*, p. 28.

24. Thomas Griffith Taylor, *Australia: A Study of Warm Environments and Their Effect on British Settlement* (London: Methuen & Co., 1940).

25. A. Grenfell Price, *White Settlers and Native Peoples: An Historical Study of Racial Contact between English-Speaking Whites and Aboriginal Peoples in the United States, Canada, Australia, and New Zealand* (Melbourne: Georgian House; Cambridge: At the University Press, 1950), chap. 6. For a recent analysis, "The Price of Progress: Native People on the European Frontiers of Australia, New Guinea, and North America," see Wilbur R. Jacobs, *Dispossessing the American Indian* (New York: Charles Scribner's Sons, 1972), chap. 11.

26. Harper, "Turner the Historian," p. 78.

27. G. V. Portus, "Americans and Australians," *Australian Quarterly* 14 (June 1942): 30–41.

28. Price agrees with me (*White Settlers and Native Peoples*, p. 99). Allen disagrees when he writes, "If the record of the Canadian government was the best in the English-speaking world in its alleviation of the cruelties wrought by the frontiersmen upon the natives, it is perhaps not unfair to say that of the United States was the worst" (*Bush and Backwoods*, pp. 24–25).

29. See note 18.

30. Geoffrey Blainey, Australia's foremost authority on the mining industry, has written extensively and effectively: see, for example, "Gold and Governors," *Historical Studies: Australia and New Zealand* 9 (May 1961): 337–350, and "The Gold Rushes: The Year of Decision," *Historical Studies: Australia and New Zealand* 10 (May 1962): 129–140.

31. Geoffrey Blainey, *The Rush That Never Ended: A History of Australian Mining* (Melbourne: Melbourne University Press, 1963); G. Spencer Compton, "Searching Eastward for Gold in Western Australia, 1887–1896," *Journal and Proceedings of the Royal Australian Historical Society* 40 (1957): 1–44.

32. Geoffrey Blainey, *The Rise of Broken Hill* (Melbourne: Macmillan of Australia, 1968); idem, *Mines in the Spinifex: The Story of Mount Isa Mines* (Sydney: Angus and Robertson, 1960); and idem, *The Peaks of Lyell* (Melbourne: Melbourne University Press, 1954).

33. John W. McCarty, "British Investment in Overseas Mining, 1820–1914," Doctoral dissertation, Cambridge University, 1961; John

Bustin, "The Western Australian Gold Fields, 1892–1900: The Investors and Their Grievances," *Historical Studies: Australia and New Zealand* 6 (November 1954): 282–289.

34. Brian Fitzpatrick, "The Big Man's Frontier and Australian Farming," *Agricultural History* 21 (January 1947): 8–12. Fitzpatrick incorporates his views in other studies: see *The Australian People* (Carlton, Victoria: Melbourne University Press, 1946), pp. 188–189, and *The British Empire in Australia* (Melbourne: Melbourne University Press, 1941), pp. 198–206. See also N. G. Butlin, "Company Ownership of N.S.W. Pastoral Stations," *Historical Studies: Australia and New Zealand* 4 (May 1950): 89–111. Some years ago Carter Goodrich pointed out the connection between the failure of land reform and the early tendency toward collectivism, supported by both urban industrial and rural agrarian wage earners, in the Australian labor movement. He wrote, in part, "Certainly the United States owes its individualism largely to its small man's frontier; I think it is not fanciful to suggest that Australia owes much of its collectivism to the fact that the frontier was hospitable to the large man instead" ("The Australian and American Labour Movements," *Economic Record* 4 [November 1928]: 206).

35. C. Hartley Grattam, ed., *Australia* (Berkeley and Los Angeles: University of California Press, 1947), pp. 13–14, 168; idem, *Introducing Australia* (New York: John Day Co., 1942), pp. 65–66, 70–71.

36. Fred Alexander, F. K. Crowle, and J. D. Legge, *The Origins of the Eastern Goldfields Water Scheme in Western Australia* (Nedlands: University of Western Australia Press, 1954).

37. Gordon Greenwood, *Australia: A Social and Political History* (Sydney: Angus and Robertson, 1971), p. 240.

38. J. R. Robertson, "The Western Australian Timber Industry," *University Studies in History* 3 (1957): 51–59.

39. Alan Birch, "The Sydney Railway Company, 1848–1855," *Journal and Proceedings of the Royal Australian Historical Society* 40, part 2 (1957): 49–92; G. J. Abbott, "The Introduction of Railways into New South Wales, 1846–1855," *Journal of the Royal Australian Historical Society* 52, part 1 (March 1966): 33–50.

40. Greenwood, *Australia*, pp. 109, 209.

41. Allen, *Bush and Backwoods*, pp. 73–81, provides many examples of comparison in greater detail.

42. Ward, *The Australian Legend*, pp. 235–240.

43. Harper, "Turner the Historian," p. 82.

44. Allen, *Bush and Backwoods*, pp. 67–68.

45. Alexander, *Moving Frontiers*, pp. 30–32, 34.

46. Ward, *The Australian Legend*, pp. 226–227.

47. Sterling Kernek, "Australian and American Characteristics: The Influence of Differences in Economic Prosperity and the Power of Private Business," *University Studies in History* 5 (1969): 1–31.

48. Allen, *Bush and Backwoods*, p. 98.

49. Ibid., pp. 92–101, presents a full discussion.

50. Harper, "Turner the Historian," pp. 82–83.

51. Allen, *Bush and Backwoods*, pp. 102–104.

52. Harper, "Turner the Historian," p. 83.

53. Allen, *Bush and Backwoods*, pp. 106–109.

54. Ward, *The Australian Legend*, p. 228.

55. Kernek, "Australian and American Characteristics," p. 1.

56. Sharp, "Three Frontiers," p. 371.

57. The University of Oklahoma had announced a symposium on comparative frontiers simultaneously in time with the presentation of this paper, April 1975, where specialists in anthropology, geography, and history would consider theories and methodologies and "their application to the general problem of the frontier as a focal point for social, economic and political change." Paul Sharp is president of the University of Oklahoma.

58. Norman D. Harper, "The Rural and Urban Frontiers," *Historical Studies: Australia and New Zealand* 10 (May 1963): 401–421.

59. Allen, *Bush and Backwoods*, p. 114.

60. George Nadel, *Australia's Colonial Culture: Ideas, Men, and Institutions in Mid–Nineteenth Century Eastern Australia* (Cambridge: Harvard University Press, 1957), pp. xi–xiii, 1–5, 271–275; Dietrich Gerhard, "The Frontier in Comparative View," *Comparative Studies in Society and History* 1 (March 1959): 229 n.; Mikesell, "Comparative Studies in Frontier History," p. 71. Mikesell presents the book as an example of the "metropolitan" orientation of Australian history comparable to the replacement of the "Laurentian School" in Canadian history by the "Metropolitan School."

61. Michael Roe, *Quest for Authority in Eastern Australia, 1835–1851* (Melbourne: Melbourne University Press, 1965); Timothy Sut-

ter, *Hierarchy and Democracy in Australia, 1788–1870: The Formation of Australian Catholicism* (Melbourne: Melbourne University Press, 1965); John Barrett, *That Better Country: The Religious Aspect of Life in Eastern Australia, 1835–1850* (Melbourne: Melbourne University Press, 1966).

62. Paul F. Bourke, "Some Recent Essays in Australian Intellectual History," *Historical Studies* 13 (October 1967): 97–105.

63. J. A. LaNauze, "The Study of Australian History, 1929–1959," *Historical Studies: Australia and New Zealand* 9 (November 1959): 7.

64. Harper, "The Rural and Urban Frontiers," pp. 420–421.

65. Alexander, *Moving Frontiers*, p. 33.

66. Allen, *Bush and Backwoods*, pp. 20–21, 83.

67. N. G. Butlin, "The Shape of the Australian Economy, 1861–1900," *Economic Record* 34 (March 1958): 21.

68. See, for example, N. G. Butlin, *Australian Domestic Product, Investment, and Foreign Borrowing, 1861–1939* (Cambridge: At the University Press, 1962), and *Investment in Australian Economic Development, 1861–1900* (Cambridge: At the University Press, 1964); A. R. Hall, *Australian Company Finance: Sources and Use of Funds of Public Companies, 1946–1955* (Canberra: Australian National University Press, 1956), *The London Capital Market and Australia, 1870–1914* (Canberra: Australian National University Press, 1963), and *The Stock Exchange of Melbourne and the Victorian Economy, 1852–1900* (Canberra: Australian National University Press, 1968); J. D. Bailey, *A Hundred Years of Pastoral Banking: A History of the Australian Mercantile Land and Finance Company, 1863–1963* (Oxford: Clarendon Press, 1966).

69. Gordon Greenwood and John R. Laverty, *Brisbane, 1859–1959: A History of Local Government* (Brisbane: O. L. Ziegler for the Council of the City of Brisbane, 1959); John R. Laverty, "Greater Brisbane: A Response to Problems of Metropolitan Government," *Australian Journal of History and Politics* 18 (April 1972): 34–51; Ronald Lawson, "Class or Status?—The Social Structure of Brisbane in the 1890's," *Australian Journal of History and Politics* 18 (December 1972): 344–359.

70. Alan Birch and David S. Macmillan, eds., *The Sydney Scene, 1788–1960* (Melbourne: Melbourne University Press, 1962).

71. Geoffrey Serle, *The Rush to Be Rich: A History of the Colony of

Victoria, 1883–1889 (Melbourne: Melbourne University Press, 1971), chap. 9.

72. Ronald Lawson, "The 'Bush Ethos' and Brisbane in the 1890's," *Historical Studies* 14 (April 1972): 276–283. See also Lawson's *Brisbane in the 1890's: An Australian Urban Society* (Brisbane: University of Queensland Press, 1973). Lawson elaborated upon this theme at the Association of American Historians in Boston, April 1975, in a paper entitled "Toward Demythologizing the 'Australian Legend': Turner's Frontier Thesis and the Australian Experience."

BIBLIOGRAPHICAL ESSAY

For the interested reader, there follows a brief survey of some of the more important literature on the comparison of world frontiers other than those of the United States and Australia.

As early as 1904, in proposing some neglected fields for study and methods of investigation that might lead to a reinterpretation of United States history, Frederick Jackson Turner suggested, "If with our own methods of the occupation of the frontier we should compare those of other countries which have dealt with similar problems— such as Russia, Germany, and the English colonies in Canada, Australia and Africa—we should undoubtedly find most fruitful results" (*The Significance of Sections in American History* [New York: Henry Holt and Co., 1932], pp. 18–19). For a discussion of the importance of this 1904 essay, "Problems in American History," see Ray Allen Billington's *Frederick Jackson Turner* (New York: Oxford University Press, 1973), pp. 180–181, 495. Turner's suggestion apparently fell upon deaf ears. In 1940, George Wilson Pierson, one of the most incisive critics of Turner, his students, and those who embraced his ideas, still insisted that comparative studies were necessary to test the validity of the assertion that the frontier experience had produced "American traits," such as individualism and love of liberty. Controlled comparisons with other frontiers were called for ("The Frontier and Frontiersmen of Turner's Essay: A Scrutiny of the Foundations of the Middle Western Tradition," *Pennsylvania Magazine of History and Biography* 64 [October 1940]: 478). Soon Pierson reasserted: "It now seems pertinent to suggest the extension of such comparisons . . . to the whole story of settlement or environmental adjustments in South America, Australia, Africa. Did comparable situations always produce comparable results?" ("The Frontier and American Institutions: A Criticism of the Turner Theory," *New England Quarterly* 15 [June 1942]: 251).

Scholars interested in the historical debate over the validity of the ideas of Frederick Jackson Turner should not miss a recent article by Sterling Kernek, "Pierson vs. Turner: A Commentary on the Frontier Controversy," *Historical Studies* 14 (October 1969): 3–18. Kernek concludes: "Pierson can be at least as misleading as Turner. Thus, in my view, future evaluations of Turner's hypothesis should begin by looking for his 'hard,' analytical side, before going on to search for his serious weaknesses. In other words, as a tentative working assumption, start by postulating that Turner was not a rather ridiculous, agrarian romantic propagating an academic version of the American agrarian myth. This will not make his romanticism go away, of course, but one can return to that after the frontier hypothesis has been interpreted so as to maximize its plausibility. Then the historian can better assess what there is of value in the hypothesis." (P. 18)

Herbert Heaton addressed his colleagues in the Economic History Association in 1946, urging them to end their academic isolation and examine frontiers outside the United States. His own comparative study considered the foundations for economic development of the Commonwealth countries ("Other Wests than Ours," *Tasks in Economic History*, Supplement 6 to *Journal of Economic History* [December 1946]: 50–62). Three years later Richard Hofstadter attempted a summary and synthesis of historical inquiry relative to the frontier experience in the United States in the *American Scholar*, again mentioning the need for comparative history. "If the frontier alone was a self-sufficient source of democracy and individualism," he wrote, "whatsoever institutions and ideas the frontiersmen brought with them, frontiers elsewhere ought to have a similar effect. The early frontier of seignorial Canada, the South American frontier, and the Siberian frontier should have fostered democracy and individualism" ("Turner and the Frontier Myth," *American Scholar* 18 [Autumn 1949]: 438).

Long before such criticism of historians concerned with the frontier experience, both in and outside the United States, Canadian scholars had been thinking and writing about the frontier. In 1928, Walter N. Sage had written "Some Aspects of the Frontier in Canadian History," noting the extension of the New England frontier in Nova Scotia, the conflict between Canadian fur traders and American farmers in the Ohio Valley, and the settlement of the Canadian prairies by Americans as well as Canadians (*Canadian Historical Association Report* [1928]: 62–72). Simultaneously, the geographer Isaiah Bowman and his associates were studying the practical problems of pioneer settlement on various continents. They eventually published three volumes during the 1930s: *The Pioneer Fringe* (New York: American Geographical Society, 1931); *Pioneer Settlement* (New York: American Geographical Society, 1932); and *Limits of Land Settlement* (New York: Council of Foreign Relations, 1937). In this same decade, the sociologist James S. Leyburn made an interesting comparative study in *Frontier Folkways* (New Haven: Yale University Press, 1935).

Albert L. Burt emerged as a formidable proponent of the application of the Turner thesis to Canadian history. In 1940, he presented "The Frontier in the History of New France" at a meeting of the Canadian Historical Association. Noting the modifications of feudal traits and obligations, he concluded, "It was the freedom of the frontier. This fresh and invigorating breeze from the West blew through New France as well as through the English colonies" (*Canadian Historical Association Report* [1940], p. 99; see also Albert L. Burt, "Our Dynamic Society," *Minnesota History* 13 [March 1932]: 3–23). Marcus Lee Hansen and John Bartlet Brebner adopted a continental rather than national view of land rushes in North America and described, in greater detail than Sage had done much earlier, how New Englanders moved into Nova Scotia, fanned westward into Quebec and Ontario, then were forced south into the United States by the geographic barrier of the Laurentian Shield, only to head north again into the Canadian prairies when free land became available. That the international boundary was no deterrent is shown in their *The Mingling of the Canadian and American Peoples* (New Haven: Yale University Press, 1940). Brebner expanded his thesis in *North American Triangle* (New Haven: Yale University Press, 1945). Fred Landon's *Western Ontario and the American Frontier* (Toronto: Ryerson Press;

New Haven: Yale University Press, 1941) is an excellent case study documenting Brebner's sweeping thesis. Landon suggests that the frontiersmen of upper Canada in the early nineteenth century were often immigrants from the United States with life styles quite different from those of the French Canadians. As men of enterprise, their impact was great.

With this exciting and challenging background of scholarship, Paul F. Sharp, then a young doctoral student at the University of Minnesota, launched a series of comparative frontier investigations. His initial consideration of the twentieth-century Canadian West was presented at the meeting of the American Historical Association in 1946 ("The American Farmer and the Last Best West," *Agricultural History* 21 [April 1947]: 65–74). This study became the first chapter in his book *Agrarian Revolt in Western Canada: A Survey Showing American Parallels* (Minneapolis: University of Minnesota Press, 1948). Within a year there appeared in the *American Historical Review* (55 [January 1950]: 286–300) Sharp's "When Our West Moved North," a more elaborate presentation of his theme stated in the closing sentences: "Familiarity with . . . other Wests enriches our understanding of our own West and reveals the full meaning of development that otherwise remains obscure. The history of the northern plains illustrates the relevance of this plea with particular emphasis, for the history of the trans-Mississippi West is imperfectly understood and incompletely told when we ignore the trek to the north and stop at a line which existed only on a map." Sharp later illustrated the regional unity and interrelationships between the American and Canadian plains in *Whoop-Up Country: The Canadian-American West, 1865–1885* (Minneapolis: University of Minnesota Press, 1955).

So much had been written on Canada with a Turnerian interpretation that Morris Zazlow prepared a rebuttal in 1948 emphasizing Canada's trans-Atlantic connections and the uniqueness of the Canadian environment ("The Frontier Hypothesis in Recent Canadian Historiography," *Canadian Historical Review* 29 [June 1948]: 153–167). However, the study of the Canadian frontier had reached a stage where W. A. Mackintosh and W. L. G. Joerg could successfully edit a nine-volume series with the title *Canadian Frontiers of Settlement* (Toronto: Macmillan, 1934–1940), designed to reach an audience much larger than the academic profession. Among the volumes in this series should be mentioned W. A. Mackintosh, *Prairie Settlement*; Arthur S. Morton and Chester Martin, *History of Prairie Settlement and "Dominion Lands" Policy*; C. A. Dawson, *Pioneering in the Prairie Provinces*; and A. R. M. Lower and H. A. Innes, *Settlement of the Forest and Mining Frontiers*.

Despite my concern in this bibliographical essay with the primacy of Canadian scholarship regarding the frontier experience and with the work of Australian historians in my essay, one should not minimize the comparative aspects of many other frontiers mentioned by Turner seventy years ago. Interested investigators should begin with two articles: Dietrich Gerhard's "The Frontier in Comparative View," *Comparative Studies in Society and History* 1 (March 1959): 205–229, and Marvin W. Mikesell's "Comparative Studies in Frontier History," *Annals of the Association of American Geographers* 50 (March 1960): 62–74. Gerhard, a European "Americanist" at the University of Cologne and later at Washington University in Saint Louis, reexamines aspects of the Turner thesis as applied to Canada, Australia, South Africa, Germany, and Russia. His essay is exceptionally penetrating when dealing with the eastern movement of Germans into Slavic areas in the late Middle Ages and the Russian advance into Siberia. Mikesell, a geographer, contributes a statement about the frontiers of Latin America but concentrates on Canada, Australia, and South Africa with minimal attention to Germany and Russia. A condensed version of Mikesell's article can be found in Richard Hofstadter and Seymour Martin Lipset's *Turner and the Sociology of the Frontier* (New York and London: Basic Books, 1968), pp. 152–171.

More recently, Louis Hartz's *Founding of New Societies* (New York: Harcourt, Brace & World, 1964) has presented a challenging framework for comparing frontiers. His pioneering work contains many fresh concepts and ideas.

Social scientists, particularly cultural geographers, have shown greater interest in comparative studies than have historians. Mikesell's most recent publications suggest two primary areas of research: interdisciplinary relationships and environmental concerns. Among the former, see "Geographic Perspectives in Anthropology," *Annals of the Association of American Geographers* 57 (September 1967): 617–634, and "Geography and Its Neighbors: Comments on the International Encyclopaedia of the Social Sciences," *Geographical Review* 59

(April 1969): 276–283. For environmental investigations of a comparative nature, see his "The Deforestation of Mount Lebanon," *Geographical Review* 59 (January 1969): 1–28; "Report of the Association of American Geographers Task Force on Environmental Quality," *Professional Geographer* 25 (February 1973): 39–47; and, edited with Ian R. Manners, *Perspectives on Environment: Essays Requested by the Panel on Environmental Education, Commission on College Geography* (Washington, D.C.: Association of American Geographers, 1974). Another geographer whose work has concentrated on theory and method as related to settlement patterns, including frontier areas, is John C. Hudson of Northwestern University. Two seminal works by him are, with Phillip M. Fowler, *The Concept of Pattern in Geography* (Iowa City: Department of Geography, University of Iowa, 1970) and *Geographical Diffusion Theory* (Evanston: Department of Geography, Northwestern University, 1972). Two of his recent articles consider settlement patterns on two contrasting frontiers: "Density and Pattern in Suburban Fringes," *Annals of the Association of American Geographers* 63 (March 1973): 28–39, and "Two Dakota Homestead Frontiers," *Annals of the Association of American Geographers* 63 (December 1973): 442–462.

For those concerned with South Africa, Eric A. Walker's *The Frontier Tradition in South Africa* (London: Oxford University Press, 1930) is basic. Recent revisionism can be read in S. Daniel Neumark's *The South African Frontier: Economic Influences, 1652–1836* (Stanford: Stanford University Press, 1957). A challenge to his views has been made by William Keith Hancock in "Trek," *Economic History Review*, 2d ser., 10 (April 1958): 331–339.

On South America there is Silvio Zavala's "The Frontiers of Hispanic America," in *The Frontier in Perspective*, edited by Walker D. Wyman and Clifton B. Kroeber (Madison: University of Wisconsin Press, 1957), pp. 35–58. See also Preston E. James, *Latin America* (New York: Odyssey Press, 1950), and Philip W. Powell, *Soldiers, Indians, and Silver: The Northwest Advance of New Spain, 1550–1600* (Berkeley and Los Angeles: University of California Press, 1952). Emilio Willems, a cultural anthropologist, has written extensively on social change, primarily in Brazil, his area of specialization. Among his many books, published in English and in Portuguese, investigators of the comparative frontier should see, with Giocanda

Mussolini, *Buzios Island: a Caicara Community in Southern Brazil* (Locust Valley, N.Y.: J. J. Augustin Publisher, 1952) and *Followers of the New Faith: Culture Change and the Rise of Protestantism in Brazil and Chile* (Nashville: Vanderbilt University Press, 1967). Recent notable articles by him are "Peasantry and City: Cultural Persistence and Change in Historical Perspective, a European Case," *American Anthropologist* 72 (June 1970): 528–544, and "Social Differentiation in Colonial Brazil," *Comparative Studies in Society and History* 12 (January 1970): 31–49.

Years ago James Westfall Thompson compared German colonization to the east with geographic stages and various periods of the westward movement in the United States. Among his many articles and books, those of special importance are "East German Colonization in the Middle Ages," *Annual Report of the American Historical Association for the Year of 1915*, pp. 125–150; *Feudal Germany* (Chicago: University of Chicago Press, 1928); and *Economic and Social History of the Middle Ages* (New York and London: Century Co., 1928). Gerhard's article notes the continuing work of German scholars, publishing in German, who have considered aspects of German-Slavic affairs.

Scholars interested in the Russian frontier begin with Vasily Klyuchevskii, generally recognized as the greatest of the pre-Soviet Russian historians, just as Americans start with Turner. See Michael Karpovich, "Klyuchevskii and Recent Trends in Russian Historiography," *Slavonic and East European Review* 21 (March 1943): 31–39. Siberian developments are considered in Raymond H. Fisher, *The Russian Fur Trade, 1550–1700* (Berkeley and Los Angeles: University of California Press, 1943); George V. Lantzeff, *Siberia in the Seventeenth Century* (Berkeley and Los Angeles: University of California Press, 1943); Donald W. Treadgold, "Russian Expansion in the Light of Turner's Study of the American Frontier," *Agricultural History* 26 (October 1952): 147–152, and *The Great Siberian Migration: Government and Peasant Resettlement from Emancipation to the First World War* (Princeton: Princeton University Press, 1957); and A. Lobanov-Rostovsky, "Russian Expansion in the Far East in Light of the Turner Hypothesis," in *The Frontier in Perspective*, edited by Walker D. Wyman and Clifton B. Kroeber (Madison: University of Wisconsin Press, 1957), pp. 79–94.

Walter Prescott Webb's Arid West: Four Decades Later

W. Eugene Hollon

Walter Prescott Webb maintained a love-hate relationship with the arid West for three-quarters of a century. The region helped shape his character and personality and remained a significant force throughout a long and distinguished career. No matter how far he traveled or how many honors he received late in life, he retained a spiritual attachment to the hardscrabble land where he spent his formative years.

When a friend once asked him when he started preparing for *The Great Plains*, Webb wrote:

> . . . *I began at the age of four when my father left the humid East*

and set his family down in West Texas, in the very edge of the open,
arid country which stretched north and west farther than a boy could
imagine. There I touched the hem of the garment of the real frontier;
there I tasted alkali. . . . There I saw the crops burned by drought,
eaten by grasshoppers, and destroyed by hail. I felt the searing winds
come furnace-hot from the desert to destroy in a day the hopes of a
year, and I saw a trail herd blinded and crazy from thirst completely
out of control of horse-weary cowboys with faces so drawn they looked
like death masks. . . . The whole Great Plains was there in microcosm,
and the book I wrote was but an extension and explanation of what I
had known firsthand in miniature, in a sense an autobiography with
scholarly trimmings.[1]

The Texas historian stated in this classic study that the western
half of the United States is a region of many deficiencies when compared to the East, and that beyond the ninety-eighth meridian water
is far more important than land. He was not the first to make such
an observation, for Zebulon M. Pike, Stephen H. Long, John C. Fré-
mont, John W. Powell, and a host of other western explorers implied
the same thing throughout the nineteenth century. Three hundred
years earlier, Pedro Castañeda, chronicler for the ill-fated Coronado
expedition, described the southern portion of the plains as a great desert, and there is no reason to believe that the Spaniard did not recognize one when he saw it.

In 1821, Maj. Stephen H. Long fixed the name "Great American
Desert" on that part of the West between the ninety-eighth meridian
and the Rocky Mountains. He thought of the land beyond the Rockies
as an extension of the American desert, although the Great Basin was
not yet a part of the United States. The area that the explorer examined and thus labeled eventually came to be known as the Great
Plains. Geography books showed the limits of the desert with varying
boundaries until the 1870s, and Americans accepted it as a fact and
not a myth. As virgin land became more scarce, the arid West appeared more attractive, and from time to time false prophets aroused
hope that a desert did not exist at all or, if so, its climate could be
changed for the better.

Special interests, particularly railroad promoters and land speculators, were among the most active forces in transforming the Great

American Desert into the Great American Garden. For obvious reasons they wanted the agricultural frontier pushed out onto the plains to make room for hundreds of thousands of new settlers. Thus, they supported the idea that pioneer farmers could subsist beyond the ninety-eighth meridian on the 160 acres of land provided for in the Homestead Act of 1862. Within a decade the desert had vanished completely from the geography books and was rarely mentioned again in many parts of the West until the middle of the twentieth century. The idea that much of the West consisted of a vast desert was "bad news" for town boosters, railroad promoters, land speculators, and settlers who wished to sell their holdings and move elsewhere.

The development of dry-farming techniques, expansion of irrigation, application of chemical fertilizers, and evolution of hybrids and drought-resistant plants helped millions of people subsist in a region that originally had been avoided like a plague by everyone but the Indians. But periodic droughts, such as the ones in the late 1880s, early 1930s, and throughout the 1950s, would prove that it was easier to abolish a desert in name than in fact.

Webb stated in 1931 that not enough water existed in the region of more than a billion acres to go around and that science had been unable to perform the miracle that Jesus accomplished with only five loaves and two fish. The Texas historian never tried to duck a controversial issue, but he did not yet classify the Great Plains as a desert. "It does not make a writer popular to speak of the shortcomings and deficiencies of a country," he wrote, "and to do so is to bring down upon one a local storm of adverse criticism. Even the scientist has to apologize for designating certain regions as arid or semi-arid, and some of them have used the term 'sub-humid' in order to shield themselves from the local critics."[2]

In literally hundreds of lectures and dozens of public speeches and articles between 1931 and 1963, Webb emphasized variations of the same theme, namely, that the amount of moisture available for the entire Great Plains could not support large oasis cities and irrigation indefinitely. He expanded this theme in his *The Great Frontier* to include the major arid regions of the world. In 1954 he produced the small volume *More Water for Texas*. In the introduction of this highly significant work, the author provided an interesting insight into a lifelong obsession with land and water. "I grew up in central West

Texas," he explained, "where there was barely enough water for domestic purposes, often not enough for the stock, and never enough for the crops except in the unusual years when the rains came in bountiful supply. In nearly every yard . . . stood one or two barrels in which water was hauled from the nearest scum-covered pond, or, if you were lucky enough to live close, some itinerant creek pool. When the barrel was filled, it was covered with heavy canvas, usually a worn-out cotton sack, and this was held in place by slipping an iron hoop down, making the canvas tight like a drumhead. The canvas would become wet with the sloshing of the precious liquid, and from this constant wetting and drying, it took on an odor of decaying cloth and parched alkali from evaporating hard water, an odor that lingers long in the nostrils."[3] Years later the historian observed that "when the rain came it made everyone happy. I loved to hear it on the roof; yet I could not understand why the sound of it made a lump come in my throat. It still does."[4]

In 1946 Webb came for a lecture to the University of Oklahoma where I was a junior member of the Department of History. After an all-night train ride he immediately went to a motel room to relax alone for a few hours. When I came for him later that evening, he wore only an old-fashioned pair of BVDs—the first time I had ever seen him without a coat and tie. He apologized for not being ready and explained that he had gotten interested in a new copy of the *Saturday Evening Post* and had let the time slip by. As he started to dress, the thought came to mind that he and Herbert Hoover had more in common than I had ever realized. Hoover must have been the last American to abandon the high celluloid collar, and Webb was probably the last one who still wore one-piece cotton drawers, flap and all.

During the next ten or fifteen minutes in that motel room approximately three decades ago, I learned more about the man in many ways than in the previous ten years: "I like the solitude of a motel room in a strange town whereby I can lie down with a copy of the *Post* or *Harper's*, stripped to my underwear, and read and think," he said. "It is even more pleasant when I can hear the sound of rain, for the first truly original idea I ever had came to me on a dark winter night a long time ago. A heavy rain was rattling on the roof of the small back room where I was trying to write an article." He then went on to talk briefly about how he had stumbled across the idea that later became the thesis of his *The Great Plains*. It made such a profound impression at the time that I can still recall his remarks word for word.

While re-reading Webb's presidential address delivered before the American Historical Association in 1958, I recently came upon the same account of the experience that he had described to me a dozen years earlier: "[The] idea that something important happened when the Americans came out of the woods and undertook to live on the plains freed me from authority, and set me out on an independent course of inquiry," he wrote. "One question I asked over and over, of myself and of others: . . . What . . . changes took place in the manner of living when thousands of west-bound people emerged from a humid, broken woodland to live on the level, semi-arid plains where there was never enough water and practically no wood? This question attended me in all my reading . . . as I studied the Western environment and tried to find its effects on human beings."[5]

Those familiar with the thesis of Webb's *The Great Plains* know that he obviously found logical answers to various questions that he initially had raised. Western historians generally agree today that this book represents the most original and significant idea about the American West that has appeared since Frederick Jackson Turner delivered his famous essay on the influence of the frontier at the Chicago World's Fair in 1893.[6] The annual sales of Webb's first book about the West have never fallen below five hundred copies, and it has never been revised. If the treatment of some subjects appears dated and superficial to young historians today, they must remember that Webb originated many ideas that are now taken for granted. A trail blazer who took facts that others had dug up, he used them as mental tools to shape and polish his original abstractions. When J. Frank Dobie wrote that "Webb never let facts stand in the way of truth," he was being complimentary and not facetious.

The Texas historian drew heavily upon childhood experiences in his classroom lectures, but never in a maudlin or overly sentimental fashion. His attraction to the poignant stories of Hamlin Garland, John Steinbeck, and Dorothy Scarborough obviously resulted from an ability to relate to the characters in their works. While describing the climate of the High Plains, he sometimes would mention Scarborough's novel *The Wind*, a story of a farm wife living in West Texas in the 1920s who was driven to a nervous breakdown by hard work, incessant wind and sand, and eternally depressing loneliness.[7] Webb especially admired "A Day's Pleasure," a moving story in Garland's *Main Travelled Roads* and probably one of the most realistic descriptions ever written of the grim existence of a farm family on the northern plains.[8] Garland described one chilly fall day in the life of a farm woman who accompanied her husband and youngest child into town in an open wagon. Her thin body shivered from the strong wind, and her drawn, leathery face and stooped shoulders made her appear twenty years older than her true age. Once they arrived in town and in front of the grocery store, the country woman felt greatly embarrassed by her faded dress and worn-out shoes. She wanted to buy enough material to patch the children's clothes for winter. But she quickly discovered that her money would not go far enough, and in the end she came away with only some cotton flannel, mittens, and a spool of thread.

While her husband visited and joked with friends at the blacksmith shop and the feed store, the wife timidly strolled up one side of the main street and down the other. Finally, she ventured into the nearby residential area of white houses and flower gardens, surrounded by freshly painted picket fences. Suddenly, a young housewife hurried out on the walk, introduced herself as "Mrs. Hall," and invited the stranger in for a brief rest and a cup of tea. Never had the farm woman seen such beautiful wallpaper, white lace curtains, elegant piano and pictures, or such speckless floors. She tried desperately to respond to small talk but had not seen another woman for so long that words proved difficult to form. The kindness and sympathy in Mrs. Hall's voice brought tears to her eyes—tears that seemed to cool her eyes and clear her mind. For weeks after she returned home later that evening, she continued to live vicariously in the neat white house in town.

After he had read *The Grapes of Wrath* and seen the movie, Webb was saddened to realize that some Americans lived such wretched and poverty-stricken lives as those of the Joad family. As a boy he had seen their counterparts pass his parents' farm on the edge of the Great Plains, en route in canvas-topped wagons to the general area of the Texas Panhandle. A cow invariably was tied to the back, and a few chickens, household furniture, and perhaps a plow were loaded in the wagon with the wife and parcel of kids. A hound dog or two brought up the rear. A college schoolmate of mine used to describe his boyhood in East Texas, where his father tried to scratch out a living as a sharecropper. "My old man moved so often from tenant farm to tenant farm," he would drawl, "that, every time he backed the wagon up to the front porch, the dogs would run and hide, and the chickens would automatically cross their legs in order to be tied up."

Within a year or two, young Walter might recognize the same families passing his house again, this time headed toward the east. "One could always tell which direction a wagon train was going by what the occupants left behind where they had camped," he would say with a sly grin. "If there were a lot of tin cans and paper sacks, the travelers invariably were on their way west. But, if the ground was covered with field-lark feathers and rabbit fur, then you knew that some more dry-land farmers had gone 'busted' and were headed back east to live with the wife's kinfolks."

New students were always slightly uncertain what to expect from the dour-looking professor, but it did not take long to discover that behind those rimless glasses and brusque expression was a laconic wit as dry as the sand hills of West Texas, yet as fresh as a summer breeze. No one received more pleasure from a humorous anecdote, and any story about the climate in West Texas especially brought forth a hearty laugh. On such occasions, Webb's eyes would light up and wrinkles would appear on the upper portion of his face, then suddenly race all the way to the top of his bald head. A student became an instant success if he could edge in quickly with an apt anecdote during a pause in the lecture. Once, during a discussion of droughts on the Great Plains, a member of the class injected the old bromide about a man in Odessa who fainted and had to be revived with a bucket of sand. The professor doubtless had heard that one a dozen times, but one would never know it by the genuine laughter that followed. On another occasion someone asked him what he thought about people in West Texas who went to church to pray for rain yet had such little faith that they did not bother to take umbrellas. He responded that praying, firing off cannons, or hanging snakes belly-up on fences brought rain sooner or later, but only during very wet seasons.

Westerners have tried all sorts of nostrums to obtain sufficient moisture to grow crops, but only irrigation proved halfway reliable year in and year out. The Mormons used it on a limited scale before 1850, and long before the end of the nineteenth century it seemed to fulfill the old dream of making the desert blossom. Webb wrote in his *The Great Plains* that "the yield on the irrigated strip is marvelous to behold; but one cannot lose sight of the millions of acres lying back from the river, for which there is no water for irrigation purposes."[9] He also maintained that unrestricted pumping of underground water in various sections of the Great Plains would eventually prove disastrous. Irrigation farming, he said, "has attracted more attention from the national government and from the public than any other single item of National Conservation. It has been magnified out of all proportion to results, if not beyond its absolute importance. As a national enterprise it has so far proved unprofitable, if not a failure."[10] More than three decades would pass before this blunt assessment began to take on the characteristics of grim reality.

In 1931, the Great Plains region entered another period of below-normal rainfall and a dust bowl soon covered it from Canada to the Mexican border. Practically the only farmers who survived those ugly years were those who used stream water or exploited the great aquifers, the subterranean water-bearing formations that underlay large portions of the arid West. By the end of the decade rains had returned, and the vast region forming the eastern slope of the Rockies became a breadbasket of the western world. It appeared once again that the old biblical proverb about making the "desert blossom like the crocus" had come true. Moreover, Webb's pessimistic opinion on the long-range effects of irrigated farming seemed ludicrous.

The amount of land in irrigation in the eleven Great Plains states increased from approximately seven million acres in the mid-thirties to more than twenty million by the mid-sixties, inadvertently helping create one of the nation's greatest domestic problems—farm surpluses.[11] The most rapid expansion of irrigation acreage came between 1950 and 1954 during the height of another severe drought. But West Texas farmers remained confident that the Ogallala aquifer would support their crops indefinitely.[12] This formation contained water put there thousands of years previously, and most farmers seemed unconcerned when the water level began to drop at the rate of 2.8 feet per year, compared to the approximately one-half inch that nature replenished annually.[13]

Long before, Webb had turned his attention to research and writing about other topics. In 1935, *The Texas Rangers* appeared, followed two years later by *Divided We Stand*. But, with the approach of another long dry cycle, the historian renewed his interest in the subject of water. He reached a national audience in the December 1953 issue of *Harper's Magazine* with an article entitled "Billion-Dollar Cure for Texas' Drought." Webb got straight to the point: "Water is today the most valuable asset in Texas—more valuable than oil, or cattle, or cotton, or any other commodity."[14] The Texas historian then described the conditions existing throughout the Great Plains after two or three years with virtually no rain. Almost every community rationed water, rivers no longer flowed, springs dried up, and pumps reached deeper and deeper for irrigation water.

A partial solution to the problem, according to Webb, was a billion-dollar plan developed by the United States Corps of Engineers to divert surplus waters from humid East Texas to the arid plains between San Antonio and the Lower Rio Grande Valley via a complex of dams and canals. He warned that, unless bold projects of this type were started at once, a crisis would threaten some regions during the next fifteen years and would spread throughout most of the Great Plains.

Webb expanded the *Harper's* article into a small book, which appeared a few months later under the title *More Water for Texas: The Problem and the Plan*. He reiterated that residents of the High Plains would have to reduce irrigation or else cities and industry would suffer the consequences. The alternative would be to divert water from humid areas to nearby arid sections as quickly as possible. The article aroused considerable interest, but, as soon as the drought ended, Texans gratefully turned to other problems and pleasures. Such cities as Dallas and Fort Worth profited greatly by their experience, however, and ultimately completed construction of several new reservoirs as security against a future shortage. The newly created Lake Meredith on the Canadian River also soon supplemented the water supply of Lubbock, Amarillo, and other Panhandle cities.

By the time of Webb's death in 1963, some West Texans realized that the Ogallala aquifer could not last forever. "Every year or so, farmers watered fewer rows at each 'set,' lowered their pumps, and drilled more wells, which produced less water than their original wells," Donald Green wrote in his recently published *Land of the Underground Rain.*[15] But for many farmers it was already too late to heed Webb's warning and start conserving ground water. As the situation worsens today, knowledgeable observers predict that these serious problems will become unmanageable before the early 1980s—unless some form of rescue is forthcoming. The High Plains will then revert to dry-land farming and ranching of an earlier era. Today, as one drives from Lubbock to Abilene, it appears that half the farmland along Highway 84 has already returned to tumbleweeds and desert shrubs.

To state that Webb represented a lone voice crying in the wilderness about the inexorable effects of irrigated farming in the arid West would do injustice to hundreds of hydraulic engineers, geologists, and other concerned individuals. Yet, few could reach a larger audience through magazine articles and books. In addition, his reputation and prestige as the state's foremost historian and original thinker assisted greatly in drawing crowds wherever he appeared for a public lecture. Unfortunately, those who needed his message usually were not present. The average West Texas farmer never trusted a professor anyway, and few listened to one whom they believed "lived in an ivory tower."

No individuals are more generous, friendlier, or more politically conservative than the typical West Texans, who oppose so-called governmental interference with the conviction of a religious zealot. As consistent defenders of the free enterprise system, it is more than slightly ironic that "those same people who were arguing against government encroachment on their rights are now pleading with the government to interfere with their rights, and the rights of everybody else in Texas and Louisiana, to the tune of $20 billion and a 1400 mile ditch across both states."[16] Most of the money will have to come from the federal government if the plan proposed by the Corps of Engineers and the Bureau of Reclamation is ever adopted. It envisions a complex of pipelines, canals, reservoirs, and pumping stations to transport surplus water from Louisiana and East Texas to the High Plains of West Texas and eastern New Mexico. On August 5, 1969, Texas voters narrowly defeated a $3.5 million bond issue to provide funds for the construction of the initial portion of this network.

Residents of the High Plains expressed bitter disappointment at the outcome of the election, since they clearly understood that without imported water they would go broke. In the December 1974 issue of *Texas Monthly*, Gregory Curtis stated that the "plan has a death grip on their imagination and energy. . . . They are like the ancient Byzantines," he declared, "who, when their city was surrounded, sat by the thousands in the cathedrals praying for deliverance. They were not delivered."[17]

The recent plan to transport surplus water to the arid sections of the state is similar to the idea that Webb proposed two decades earlier. As far back as 1931, he predicted that a system of canals inevitably would transport water from the Missouri or the Mississippi to cities and farms throughout the Great Plains. This was before the average individual had even heard the word *ecology*, an important factor in the defeat of the Texas bond issue in 1969. Today more people realize that the cure for one of nature's deficiencies often creates a greater problem than it solves. Webb did not have the advantage of hindsight that our generation possesses. Even if the billions of dollars required to construct such a complex were available, conservationists probably could defeat the idea.

Walter Prescott Webb was a very kind, gentle individual who never sought a controversy or a quarrel, yet they invariably seemed to follow in his wake. With the exception of *The Texas Rangers*, each of his major books aroused strong opposition and criticism immediately upon publication. *The Great Frontier* has not yet gained the status of *The Great Plains*, but the author believed that it ultimately would be considered his greatest work. On the other hand, *The Texas Rangers* aroused no hostility at first but has since been attacked vehemently by some minority groups as an insult to Indians and Mexican-Americans.[18]

Nothing that the Texas historian ever wrote aroused more instant controversy than a provocative article that appeared in the May 1957 issue of *Harper's Magazine* entitled "The American West—Perpetual Mirage." The author later explained that his purpose was to put on paper a basic truth about the American West—that at the heart of the region beyond the Mississippi lies a vast desert of varying intensity. It covers most of the eight Rocky Mountains states, plus considerable portions of the six Great Plains states on its east flank and of California, Oregon, and Washington on its west flank. The desert therefore constitutes the core and is the most prominent feature of an immense arid region.[19]

Webb tried to change the focus of the West by approaching it from the center, rather than from the outside. He saw the desert as the "dominant force in shaping, conditioning, or determining much that lies within its sphere of aridity."[20] The desert influence, therefore, made water more important than land, which existed in abundance because of subnormal rainfall and a high rate of evaporation. People naturally have settled in cities near water, such as Denver, Salt Lake City, Albuquerque, Phoenix, Tucson, Reno, Boise, and Las Vegas. Webb concluded that, as these places continued to grow, they pushed harder and harder on the water supply, exhausting the amount for further industrial, agricultural, or urban expansion. He also detailed various cultural deficiencies to show that the desert influence extended to everything, including the people and their history. This latter reference made some westerners extremely angry.[21]

Mark Twain once remarked that the reason Americans became so furious when the English novelist Frances Trollope published her *Domestic Manners of the Americans* in 1832 was because she told the truth. Perhaps the same could be said about the 1957 *Harper's* article, for United States senators, governors, newspaper editors, chamber of commerce directors, and literally hundreds of average westerners immediately fired off angry letters and telegrams to the publisher or the author. They attacked Webb personally for insulting the people of the West, and some denied that a desert existed at all or they declared that their state should not be included in the so-called Great American Desert.

No western newspaper was more vociferous in denouncing the Texan than the *Denver Post*. Its editor reacted as if the word *desert* were synonymous with *sin* and *communism*: "Listen, Dr. Walter Prescott Webb, historian of the University of Texas, you better take off your glasses and your Ph.D. You've picked yourself a fight."[22] After insinuating that the ivory-towered professor might have difficulty pouring rain water out of a boot with the directions written on the heel, the *Post* editor then boasted of Colorado's tremendous growth in population and industry, its invigorating climate, clear skies, breath-taking scenery, and friendly inhabitants. With other self-appointed champions of the region, he declared that there was no water short-age in the West and, even if there were, westerners would solve their own problems as they always had.

Webb must have received satisfaction four years later from a sec-ond *Denver Post* editorial. It concerned a White House conference on natural resources recently held in Denver, during which various "out-siders" stated flatly that the West was indeed a desert. The same edi-tor who had once attacked the Texas historian with bitter sarcasm now wrote "it's time that we quit kidding ourselves." He then recalled the storm that arose over the *Harper's Magazine* article in 1957 and admitted frankly that Professor Webb had been right all along. "With the current planning and expenditures in resources management on the part of local, state, and federal government, the desert climate becomes a positive advantage to growth. It is almost like having your cake and eating it too," he concluded.[23]

A severe drought visited eastern Colorado in 1964 and spread hori-zontally and vertically across large sections of the Great Plains. Sev-eral national television programs publicized the plight of farmers and ranchers and indicated that the Great American Desert had once again become a reality. When President Lyndon Johnson eventually declared the region a national disaster area, one did not hear any com-plaints from westerners about governmental interference.

Throughout the years after World War II, thousands of Americans discovered the charm of the desert, a development that naturally pleased local land promoters, "fast-buck" artists, and chamber of com-merce officials. At the same time, a powerful mystique about the mountains has sprung up, and not since the gold- and silver-rush days of the last century have so many people migrated to the heart-land of the West. By 1970, Colorado attracted approximately fourteen hundred new residents each week, while Denver advanced along the Front Range toward the New Mexico border in one direction and to southern Wyoming in another. Ski resorts sprang up by the hundreds along the mountain slopes from southern New Mexico to northern Montana, as land promoters laid out new satellite cities by the dozens—at least on paper. The future looked bright as westerners contemplated vast profits from the rich deposits of shale oil, coal, and natural gas. The region that Webb had labeled the heart of the American desert now seemed to be having its cake and enjoying it too.

But newcomers, who had fled California's smog and traffic congestion or the urban sprawl and crime of eastern cities, realized that they had created the same environment from which they had escaped. Cities long famous for clear skies, safe streets, quiet neighborhoods, and a relaxed life style soon became unrecognizable. Phoenix, formerly a haven for asthma and hay-fever sufferers, developed one of the highest pollen counts in the country, and giant gasification and electrical plants built by El Paso Natural Gas and Utah Power and Light Company in the Four Corners area spewed approximately 350 tons of sulphur dioxide each day into the southwestern atmosphere, more than in New York and Los Angeles combined.[24]

The steel plant at Provo, Utah, and the phosphate plants in southern Idaho deposited a dirty veil of pollutants upon the magnificent Tetons in northwest Wyoming, destroying trees, vegetation, and wildlife. The more water that Denver piped from the western slope through the central Rockies, the more people and automobiles it attracted.[25] Today, the Colorado capital has the dubious distinction of possessing the nation's highest level of carbon monoxide pollutants, followed closely by Albuquerque, Salt Lake City, Tucson, and Phoenix. Main streets leading from interstate exits toward business districts of western cities are lined with garish neon signs, telephone and electric-power poles, pizza parlors, Colonel Sanders' fried chicken emporiums, Dairy Queen drive-ins, Holiday Inns, McDonald's hamburger palaces, and four filling stations at each intersection.[26]

While oasis cities in the Great American Desert suffer from increased pollution, crime, traffic jams, and urban sprawl, the countryside is being scarred by strip mining, subdivisions, condominiums, ski lodges, and vacation homes. Thousands of acres of valuable ranch, farm, and desert land have given way to concrete, asphalt, and shopping centers. At the same time the desert is being butchered by subdividers peddling worthless land without water to suckers at several thousand dollars per acre. Where water is unavailable, the land simply cannot support human habitation, and fragile desert lands broken up for roads and streets do not heal easily.

New cities surveyed for populations of 50,000 to 100,000 have sprung up in each of the desert states with little regulation by legislatures. Subdivisions in Colorado increased between 1961 and 1971 from 30 to more than 300, or enough building sites for 12 million newcomers. Lots have been sold on a large plat north of Flagstaff to accommodate a city of 50,000 people; this is only one of Arizona's 182 subdivisions with a total population capacity of 3.5 million. Mohave County alone has 46 subdivisions, which represent enough sites for twenty-two times its present population. After several years, many of these so-called satellite cities do not have a single resident. Yet, in state after state, realtors continue to sell land without water at exorbitant prices.

The recent energy shortage has focused considerable attention on the heartland of the desert. Great conglomerates have leased millions of acres of coal and shale-oil lands for strip mining. At the same time they have constructed or are building giant electrical power and gasification complexes. Former sleepy communities, such as Coalstrip, Montana, and Rock Springs, Wyoming, are undergoing cultural shocks, while lifetime residents find themselves strangers in their own communities. As thousands of workers move in, desert ghettos proliferate, taxes increase three- and fourfold, and crime, divorce, and inflation run rampant. Westerners learn that progress can be a four-letter word.

Although Webb predicted that the arid regions would soon deplete underground water supplies unless conservation methods were adopted immediately, westerners generally remained confident a decade ago that they would find permanent solutions to this problem. We had not yet put a man on the moon, but the "we can do anything" syndrome was still part of the American creed. Scientists in the Office of Saline Water Conversion held out promises that salty and brackish waters could be converted economically into pure "mother's milk." Officials in the Bureau of Land Management and the Bureaus of Reclamation and Engineers studied such projects as the 100 billion dollar NAWAPA plan (North American Water and Power Alliance), whereby surplus water from Alaska would be channeled into the arid West by a complex of dams, reservoirs, pipelines, and canals. Others talked about improving the techniques of cloud seeding, checking evaporation waste on giant reservoirs, and even towing icebergs from the Arctic to West Coast cities as a source of fresh water.

Today, all these hopes and dreams more or less lie shattered and westerners must face grim reality. The NAWAPA plan proved as impractical as spinning chicken feathers into wool. No significant breakthrough has occurred in water conversion since 1965, while the tremendous increase in energy cost has complicated the problem. Checking rapid evaporation of impounded water with a chemical film proved less than sensational, and cloud seeding only worked where heavily laden moisture clouds existed in the atmosphere. Moreover, increased influence of such organizations as the Sierra Club and Friends of the Earth has to be reckoned with, and environmentalists can no longer be dismissed as "crackpots" and "butterfly chasers." If the list of setbacks is not already long enough, there is also the probability that large multipurpose dams will no longer be constructed on western streams.[27]

As demands for water in the West reach crisis proportions, quality and quantity have declined dramatically. The Colorado River, for example, has practically reached threshold limits for irrigation purposes in the lower-basin states. The upper-basin states of the Great American Desert annually dump an average of seventy tons of pollutants per square mile into the river. This, combined with what is picked up as the Colorado winds its way through the Grand Canyon en route to the Gulf of California, compounds the amount of sedimentation. The last United States user gets water of 900 ppm (parts per million), while the first users in Mexico get water of 1,240 ppm —240 ppms beyond which most crops will grow.[28]

The Colorado is the forerunner of what will happen sooner or later to rivers of the Great Plains, especially the Arkansas, Platte, Rio Grande, Yellowstone, and Missouri. Half the pollution of these streams comes from natural phenomena, but irrigated farming—which consumes about 80 percent of the water used in the West—exceeds all other man-made factors combined. Cities are relatively minor causes in comparison with fertilizers and pesticides applied by farmers and ranchers, plus undesirable minerals brought to the surface by irrigation pumps. Overgrazing, excessive cutting of timber, and the tremendous increase of feedlots throughout the West also contribute to pollution. (According to the Office of Environmental Protection, one cow or steer in a feedlot produces 3.6 tons of waste.)

In many ways, irrigation has been the salvation of the arid West and a major factor in making the United States the leading food and fiber producer in the world. But westerners now realize what other civilizations learned previously: they cannot flood land indefinitely without ruining it. Thousands of once-productive acres in Arizona, southern California, and northern New Mexico have become so leached of proper minerals and so saturated with salts that they now lie abandoned. Tumbleweeds, junipers, and desert scrub have taken over where vegetables, fruits, or cotton grew in abundance a few years ago. Again, there simply is not enough water in the arid West to supply the growing cities, new energy plants, strip-mining operations, and irrigation farming. One or more inexorably will have to give way to the others.[29]

The average westerner does not need another string of horror stories or gloomy predictions at this time. Indeed, there is more than enough bad news already, with the avalanche of current disasters, such as the economy, the recent involvement in Vietnam, threat of war in the Middle East, energy shortage, inflation, corporate greed, and political corruption—not necessarily in that order. Residents of the arid West have their own special problems to add to these, and they find themselves more frustrated and divided than ever. Realizing they cannot recapture things as they were, they are struggling desperately against being turned into "the backyard for the rest of the nation." They naturally resent being "ripped off" by the Hydra-headed corporate monsters who scar their landscape, pollute their air and water, and destroy their natural heritage, yet they lack the political power to match that of the East and the South.

Fortunately, the battle has not yet been completely lost. In the election of 1974, every successful gubernatorial and United States senatorial candidate in the western states was elected on a strong conservation platform. It was *the* issue in Colorado, the most ecologically concerned state in the nation, where politicians, university presidents, and even some chamber of commerce directors are advocating zero population growth. Ironically, the region that traditionally welcomed newcomers, and where few remained strangers very long, now greets visitors with bumper stickers or crude lettering on barns that read:

"Don't Californicate Colorado," "Had You Rather Eat Coal than Food?" or "Texans Go Home."

More than forty years ago, Walter Prescott Webb stated that practically every institution that settlers carried with them beyond the ninety-eighth meridian was either broken, remade, or else greatly altered: ". . . east of the Mississippi civilization stood on three legs—land, water, and timber; west of the Mississippi not one but two of these legs were withdrawn—water and timber—and civilization was left on one leg—land."[30]

Despite this gloomy observation and his parents' struggle for survival near the line that separates the semiarid from the arid region, Webb always remained optimistic about the country and the resourcefulness of its people. While pointing out the many problems and deficiencies of the arid West, he believed that these factors exerted a powerful influence in shaping the westerner's unique character. He understood more than most that mere existence required constant adjustment and change and that, in a metaphorical sense, man would always remain a trespasser in the arid West. Each time man forgets this basic fact of life about the region Mary Austin has called "the land of little rain," nature reminds him with dramatic and often tragic consequences.

NOTES

1. Walter Prescott Webb, "History as High Adventure," *American Historical Review* 64 (January 1959): 273–274.
2. Walter Prescott Webb, *The Great Plains* (Boston: Houghton Mifflin Co., 1936), p. 321.
3. Walter Prescott Webb, *More Water for Texas: The Problem and the Plan* (Austin: University of Texas Press, 1954), p. 1.
4. Ibid.
5. Walter Prescott Webb, *An Honest Preface and Other Essays* (Boston: Houghton Mifflin Co., 1959), ed. Joe B. Frantz, p. 202.
6. The Texas historian did not read Turner, incidentally, until after he had completed *The Great Plains*.

7. Dorothy Scarborough, *The Wind* (New York: Harper & Brothers, 1925).

8. Hamlin Garland, *Main Travelled Roads* (New York: Harper & Brothers, 1891), pp. 247–256.

9. Webb, *The Great Plains*, p. 333.

10. Ibid., pp. 349–350.

11. *Agricultural Statistics*, 1973 (Washington, D.C.: U.S. Government Printing Office), p. 427.

12. Donald E. Green, *Land of the Underground Rain: Irrigation on the Texas High Plains, 1910–1970* (Austin: University of Texas Press, 1973), p. 148. This is especially true in the region of the Texas High Plains, where the number of wells increased from 14,000 to 27,500.

13. John Graves, "The Hard-Used Land," *Atlantic* 235 (March 1975): 91.

14. Walter Prescott Webb, "Billion-Dollar Cure for Texas' Drought," *Harper's Magazine* 207 (December 1953): 76.

15. Green, *Land of the Underground Rain*, p. 191.

16. Gregory Curtis, "Disaster, Part I: Lubbock Is Running Out of Water," *Texas Monthly* 2 (December 1974): 81.

17. Ibid., p. 97.

18. Calling the author a racist, as some have done, is absurd and applies standards of the present to the past in a simplistic reinterpretation of history.

19. Walter Prescott Webb, "The West and the Desert," *Montana, the Magazine of Western History* (Winter 1958). Reprinted in Webb's *An Honest Preface*, pp. 175–193. (See also the original article in *Harper's Magazine* 214 [May 1957]: 25–31.)

20. Webb, *An Honest Preface*, p. 177.

21. Webb stated that the West had not yet produced a great statesman, that the *Dictionary of American Biography* and *Who's Who in America* contained very few sketches of westerners in comparison to Americans from other parts of the country, and that not a single western man had been voted into the American Hall of Fame. He further declared that westerners had developed a talent for taking something small—for example, their brief and bizarre history—and blowing it up to giant size like a photographer enlarges a photograph.

22. *Denver Post*, April 28, 1957.

23. Ibid., November 14, 1961.

24. Interview with Dr. John R. Bartlett, chemical engineer at Los Alamos and foremost authority on air pollution, Santa Fe, New Mexico, October 25, 1974.

25. A member of the Colorado State Planning Board estimated in 1973 that each new resident in the state would ultimately cost present taxpayers more than $20,000 in additional services.

26. John Kenneth Galbraith has remarked frequently that filling-station architecture represents the ugliest man-made work to appear in the last two thousand years; but that is not doing justice to the fast-food chains.

27. The conclusions relative to current water-development conditions in the arid West are based upon the results of a conference in the Bureau of Interior with Dave Gudgel, Assistant Special Projects Office, Bureau of Reclamation; Richard Nash, chief of reports, Coordination Branch of the Bureau of Reclamation; and John Heintz, Office of Saline Water Conversion, Washington, D.C., August 5, 1974.

28. *Colorado River International Salinity Control Project*, Special Report, September 1973, United States Department of the Interior, Bureau of Reclamation, Office of Saline Water Conversion (Washington, D.C.: U.S. Government Printing Office), p. 2.

29. It has long been known that the mountain and northern plains states contain some of the richest coal veins in the world—or an estimated 86.1 billion tons lying 50 to 100 feet below the surface and possibly worth $300 billion in gross sales to coal companies. In addition, Wyoming, Utah, and Colorado possess 300 trillion cubic feet of natural gas, held in deep sand formations, and an estimated 600 billion barrels of shale oil. At the same time, the estimated water requirement for producing 100,000 barrels of oil per day varies from 5,000 to 20,000 acre feet, depending upon mining techniques used at a particular site. Since the great conglomerates have the money and the political power, they eventually will get all the water they need, most of it at the expense of irrigation. No law or constitutional amendment has yet been passed that has regulated rich and powerful special interests out of business.

30. Webb, *The Great Plains*, p. 9.

The Webb "Great Frontier" Hypothesis and International Law

George Wolfskill

On July 29, 1955, President Dwight D. Eisenhower caught the attention of the entire world when he announced that the United States, as a part of its program for the International Geophysical Year, planned to launch a satellite into earth orbit. But the Soviet Union beat him to it, and the space age became a reality on October 29, 1957, with the successful launch of Sputnik I.

A corollary to that dramatic event was the legal ramification of man in space. For nearly two decades since Sputnik I, international space law has been a matter of legitimate concern to both governments and legal scholars. The thrust of most of the literature on international space law has been that of applying, by analogy, existing law to conditions in space. In 1952, well before Sputnik I, Oscar Schachter, then deputy director of the United Nations Legal Department, anticipated what would probably happen. What, he asked rhetorically, would be the legal problems in the conquest of space? Where would one look "to find principles and precedents to answer these problems?" Schachter concluded that "we have to go back four centuries, to the great age of exploration and conquests."[1]

Schachter believed that the legal problems in space would resemble those of the great Age of Discovery; the answers would be found in analogy, in updating established principles of international law to suit a new Age of Discovery in space.

After Sputnik I, Schachter's answer became more than mere speculation: it became the basis of United States space policy. In 1961, Adlai Stevenson, then United States ambassador to the United Nations, told that body that it should "state explicitly that the rules of good international conduct" follow man "wherever he goes."[2] A year later, Senator Albert Gore of Tennessee, in a speech before that organization, observed that "outer space is not a new subject, it is a new place in which all the old subjects come up."[3]

No one summarized the United States's analogy approach better than Col. Martin Menter, judge advocate of the United States Air Force, before the Sixth Colloquium on the Law of Outer Space, held in Paris in 1963: "The law governing space activities cannot be established independently of principles of law developed to govern man's activities on earth. This does not mean that all laws on earth automatically apply to space, but that in determining the law that should apply to space activities we must reexamine analogous related laws, such as the Law of the Sea and Air Law, among others, to determine whether the underlying rationale of such law may also be applicable to the new environment of outer space."[4]

Meanwhile, American chief executives, among others, urged that a body of space law be developed as quickly as possible. In September 1960, President Dwight D. Eisenhower, in a speech before the United Nations General Assembly, challenged that body to get on with the task. "National vested interests have not yet been developed in space or in celestial bodies," said the president. "Barriers to agreement are now lower than they will ever be again."[5] President John F. Kennedy made a similar proposal predicated on the poignant question of whether space was going to be "a sea of peace or a new terrifying theater of war."[6] "Our American dream for outer space," said President Lyndon B. Johnson, "is a dream of peace. We are working and we will continue to work through the United Nations . . . to extend the rule of law into outer space."[7]

In the intervening years, a considerable body of space law has been developed, based largely, as I have already suggested, on analogy. There are, for example, the 1963 Treaty Banning Nuclear Tests in the Atmosphere; the 1967 General Treaty of Principles Governing the Activities of States in the Exploration and Use of Outer Space; the 1968 Agreement on the Rescue of Astronauts, the Return of Astronauts, and the Return of Objects Launched into Outer Space; and the 1968 Treaty for Liability for Damages Caused by Objects Launched into Outer Space.

In addition, the United Nations has passed numerous resolutions relating to activities in space, and the United States has signed more than two hundred bilateral agreements relating to a great variety of cooperative enterprises in the exploration of space. And there is also considerable activity—much more than can be listed here—in all the major countries directed toward the ultimate codification of space law.

There thus appears to be an impressive beginning in space law since the launching of Sputnik I. If historians of the twenty-first century—assuming there are any—sadly record the collapse of international law during the space age, it will not be because legal experts failed to anticipate the problems.

Despite the apparent progress in space law, something is seriously wrong with international law in our time. What gives life and vitality to any legal system, national or international, is the spirit of the law. The spirit of the law, voluntarily assumed, positively asserted, and universally self-imposed, makes legal systems effective. I believe that something significant and at the same time ominous has happened to wither the spirit of international law in the twentieth century. The legal problems of space are but a distraction, one of major proportions to be sure, but a distraction, all the same, from the real problem.

To understand what has happened to that spirit of the law in this century, it is essential to understand what made international law modern in the first place. It is not enough to say, tongue in cheek, that international law is modern because it is a recent and important by-product of the rise of the nation-state system inaugurated by the Peace of Westphalia in 1648.

International law is not modern because it is little more than three hundred years old. As one writer has said, international law did not "spring suddenly into existence like Minerva, full-grown from the head of Jove."[8] Many of the specific laws and the legal principles on which they were based evolved long before 1648. Their formal acceptance in the wake of the Congress of Westphalia merely confirmed what was already true in practice.

If international law is not modern because it is recent, or because of specific laws, or because of the legal principles underlying those laws, what, then, has made the law "modern"? At each crucial period in the history of what we now call international law, some dynamic, unifying force sustained the spirit of the law. For example, during the first major period in Rome's development its cohesive force was military might. To be perfectly candid, the law was universally effective under the Romans because of the overwhelming political power of Rome that hugged the ancient world in a strong embrace.

If the unifying force in the ancient world was the political power of Rome making universal law effective, who would carry on after the empire had been replaced by feudal provincialism? There is only one satisfactory answer. The universal nature of the Roman Catholic church made it the most important institution of the Middle Ages. Rome fell; but the church survived. And it earned its exalted place by a steadfastness when everything else reeled under the weight of the collapsing empire.

This is not the time or the place to recount the history of the church during the Middle Ages. But for approximately a thousand years— from the barbaric invasions to the emergence of the nation-state system—the church provided the centripetal force holding the nebulous mass together. For the greater part of the Middle Ages the church, as the agent of general intercourse, held all Europeans accountable to a universal law of faith and morals of which it alone was the custodian.

To return, then, to the original question: what unifying force nourished the spirit of the law and made it modern? The Dutch jurist Hugo Grotius, who published his great work *On the Law of War and Peace* in 1625, is usually credited as the father of modern international law. But why did Grotius succeed where others at least as capable had failed?

One expert, writing in the *American Political Science Review*, raised an interesting question when he asked, "Grotius, living in the midst of this seafaring people, brought up amongst the international trade of the Hollanders of those days, ought he not to have had a keener vision than a jurist of any non-trading, non-cosmopolitan country?"[9]

It is common knowledge that an incident in the commercial development and overseas expansion of his homeland, Holland, originally inspired Grotius's immortal work on the law of nations. But this might have been only coincidental. On the other hand, the writer who asked the question may have been closer to the truth than he knew. Possibly, international trade was in some way the key to the success of the Grotian system of law.

The development of nation-states and the overseas explorations that led to the discovery of the New World were contemporaneous events. At first glance, it appears that the conflicts and colonial rivalries resulting from those overseas discoveries merely accelerated the chaotic conditions of the late fifteenth and sixteenth centuries. But, although the New World discoveries accelerated the disintegration of the medieval order, they also created a wider base and a broader horizon for the development of international law.

Professor James Brown Scott claimed that the discovery of America expanded international law until it became a "universal rule of conduct."[10] There can be no quarrel with the idea that the New World discoveries broadened the concerns of the law and increased the size of the playing field over which it was to be applied, just as space exploration has done in our time. Until the New World discoveries, international law, such as it was, had been confined exclusively to Europe. The discovery of new seas and the lands beyond meant expanding the law to include the strange people inhabiting them. Europe acquired a new international outlook; and all parts of the world were brought into communication with each other in a relationship in which Europe played the dominant role.

The emancipation of Europe from the paternalism of the Roman empire and the medieval church was a prerequisite for the development of sovereign national states; and the discovery of new portions of the world offered national states unlimited opportunity for the reckless exercise of their sovereignty. The resulting lawlessness, both at home and overseas, seemed to justify the whole theory of sovereignty with its implied absence of restraints among states.

But expanding trade and commerce brought the new national states "into far more intimate and constant relations than in the days when their theoretical unity was accepted everywhere."[11] Colonial and trade rivalries accompanying the expansion of commerce resulted in endless conflicts—so many, in fact, that some men, drawn together by the compelling force of economic self-interest, realized that rules for commercial intercourse were absolutley essential.

International law became potent in European affairs when men and rulers alike understood that the economic well-being of the national state was at stake. An English jurist, Sir Robert Phillimore, grasped this point when he asserted that "the closer the bond of international intercourse became, the more urgent became the necessity for some International Law to whose decisions all members of the Commonwealth of Christendom might submit."[12] The Italian lawyer Pasquale Fiore agreed when he asserted, "Indeed, it began gradually to be understood that, in order to assure the development of national prosperity in each country, it was indispensable to facilitate the development of international relations and to guarantee and protect common interests."[13] John Westlake, one of England's most respected legal writers, reduced this important idea to the equivalent of a legal formula:

The amount of regulation which a society requires will be in proportion to the closeness of contact between its members and the complication of their mutual dealings. . . .

And the same principle has forced itself into application between states ever since the great advancement in arts and commerce, and the system established by the Peace of Westphalia under the protection of which they have flourished, has led to such intimate and constant international relations.[14]

If the subject is examined only superficially, New World discoveries at first seem merely another cause for the lawlessness that characterized international relations during the Age of Discovery. But commerce, which seldom respects national frontiers or international rivalries, creates a more sympathetic attitude toward international law. In this perspective, the American David Jayne Hill wrote, "It was in the cradle of commerce that international law awoke to consciousness."[15] Another American, Professor Julius Goebel, has echoed Hill's conclusion. "The discovery of the new world at the end of the fifteenth century," Goebel wrote, "marked the beginning of an epoch in the history of international law." "The truth of the matter," Goebel continued, "is that modern international law was forged in the fires of the economic and political struggles over colonial possessions and the control of the seas."[16]

The implications of what Hill and Goebel meant become clearer when one understands that the New World discoveries delivered a tremendous expanse of lands with little or no population into the custody of a small and densely populated Europe. And the significance of those discoveries was the influence that those new lands exerted upon the Europeans who attempted to appropriate and exploit them. With dramatic suddenness a new frontier of fantastic size had revealed itself beyond the seas—a new frontier that, with voice sweeter than any Lorelei, beckoned men to fortune, fame, and freedom.

In 1952, Walter Prescott Webb, the late professor of history at the University of Texas, published a book entitled *The Great Frontier*. In that book, Webb characterized the unusual circumstances that I have just described as a "boom," created by the abrupt disproportion of land and its wealth to population.[17] But let Webb speak for himself:

This book is based on the hypothesis that the Great Frontier as defined has been one of the primary factors in modern history. The major premise is that the sudden acquisition of land and other forms of wealth by the people of Europe precipitated a boom on Western civilization, and that the boom lasted as long as the frontier was open, a period of four centuries. A corollary of the major premise is that our modern institutions, as distinguished from medieval, were differentiated and matured during a boom, and are therefore adapted to boom conditions. . . .

. . . It was in this atmosphere and under these conditions that democracy, capitalism, and individualism of the modern type came to their dominant position.[18]

According to Webb, the New World discoveries lavished excess land and wealth in every form upon a comparatively small and fixed number of people in Europe. In Webb's "Great Frontier" hypothesis, it was the European economy that felt the first shock of New World influence. The frantic preoccupation of Europeans with the New World wealth and resources, Webb argued, eventually gave the entire age its predominantly capitalistic character.

The key word here is *capitalistic*. But, given the nature of the new national states, it was perhaps inevitable that mercantilism, not capitalism, became the dominant economic system at the outset. The state faced the overriding need of funds to pay for the armies and the administrative bureaucracy on which the power of the state depended. It is therefore understandable that the state, personified by the crown, should seek a system for monopolizing the wealth of the New World. Mercantilism, geared to producing a self-sufficient national economic unit, became the handmaiden of political absolutism.

Within this mercantilist framework, however, a great private economy was encouraged that ultimately proved the undoing of political absolutism. Yale University scholar Gerhart Niemeyer explained it this way: "Needing capital as a requisite of absolute power, Absolutism engaged in developing capitalism, which was eventually to become the cause of its downfall. Being based primarily on financial power, Absolutism took care to develop the spirit and practice of an 'acquisitive society,' thereby engendering a bourgeois mentality which soon sought to follow its own laws."[19]

By placing enormous land and wealth under the direct sovereignty of the state, the New World discoveries had created an economic condition in which the state assumed active control through a system of mercantilism that supposedly would satisfy the financial needs of the absolute ruler. But, in the process, the sovereign became increasingly dependent upon the welfare of the capitalist class, the indispensable element in the success or failure of the mercantile system.

It would be in error to claim that capitalism did not exist until the

New World discoveries. But, certainly, the capitalism of the Middle Ages was not the predominant economic characteristic of that period. Capitalism became important in the course of time when the social classes that it motivated gained power and gave to society the imprimatur that identified it as capitalistic. There can be little argument that this happened only after the New World discoveries. On this point—the triumph of capitalism—the views of Ferdinand Schevil seem worth quoting at length:

And in a society of closely interwoven parts the voyages of discovery were of necessity but a link in an unbroken chain of events. By their sensational success they redoubled the spirit of enterprise in which they had originated. The large-scale business transactions that followed necessitated correspondingly large-scale financial measures. The use of money, in place of barter, spread even to the outlying corners of Europe; and accumulated savings, put at the disposal of merchants and manufacturers, laid the solid groundwork of modern capitalism. The wealth of great cities, especially of maritime cities, registered an uninterrupted increase, and the employment of that wealth by bankers, shipbuilders, company promoters, and enterprisers of every kind gradually impressed that bourgeois or middle-class character on society which it has substantially kept down to our day.[20]

The bourgeois capitalist class took a predictable course of action. For the state to achieve its political aims through mercantilism, it had sponsored, even encouraged, capitalistic economic activities. In short, the state had sought to exploit capitalism to gain political ends. Inevitably, the course of action for the bourgeois capitalist class was to free itself from exploitation by the state.

That the bourgeois capitalist class succeeded in freeing itself from domination by the state is a familiar story. The revolutions of the seventeenth and eighteenth centuries, notably in England and France, were essentially the story of the reach for power by the bourgeois capitalist class. The scenario for that drama was neatly summarized by James Burnham in his book *The Managerial Revolution*:

The de facto alliance between prince and capitalists was dissolved, and the prince was ousted, made a figurehead, or at the least restrict-

*ed in the area of society over which his power extended. There were
more wars and revolutions, and the "ideal" bourgeois state of the late
eighteenth and nineteenth centuries emerged: political power vested
in the lower house of parliament with full assurance that the parliament was, by constitution, law, habit, custom, and belief, dedicated
to the upholding of the structure of rights and obligations in terms of
which society is organized as capitalist.*[21]

The technique by which the bourgeois capitalist class emancipated
itself from state interference at the world-wide level is not so apparent. International law provided this necessary freedom. It served a
vital need of an expanding bourgeois capitalist society. Such a system
was imperative to the capitalist class at the international level for the
same reason that domestic law on the national level was essential to
protect private property and vested interests, to assure the validity of
contracts, and to provide legal calculability in business and commercial relations.

For the capitalist class, trade and commerce are the soul of its existence. But trade and commerce depend on legal certainty. If international merchants and financiers and those related to them were to
sleep soundly and know peace of mind, the rules of the game could
not constantly change. They had to stop being terrorized by the
changing fortunes of the international struggle for power. It follows
that acceptance of international law and a standardization of that law
to assure the legal certainty of commercial relationships were essential despite the political atomization of western Europe.

I have advanced the idea—convincingly, I hope—that modern international law is related to international economics. The challenge
would be to find an international economic force so powerful that it
overshadowed all others, that would, in relation to the law, serve the
same unifying purpose and produce a comparable spirit as political
power and religion had done in earlier periods of the law.

Was there such a force? The answer is that only the New World
discoveries were of such magnitude. I agree with Professor Webb, who
argued so persuasively that after 1500 the New World discoveries
were the decisive factor in the spectacular rise of capitalism and its

practitioners. Let us take another brief look at Webb's argument: "The view advanced here is that the frontier [the Great Frontier] furnished the setting for and supplied the matrix from which capitalism grew. It furnished the substance with which capitalism works; it supplied the gold and silver which facilitated exchange; and it gave the room for that constant expansion which seems so necessary in a capitalist economy."[22]

It is clear why the system of law proposed by Hugo Grotius formed the foundation for modern international law. The bourgeois capitalists eventually became the dominant class in society; the Grotian system was one suited to the economic needs of that class. The nineteenth century became the golden age of international law because both national and international society had, by that time, been made over in the capitalist image. The spirit born in the New World discoveries and nourished by an interrelated and interdependent bourgeois capitalist society made international law effective and made it modern.

If my hypothesis is correct, the current dilemma in international law becomes apparent. Let me put it in the form of other questions. Has the influence of the bourgeois capitalist class and its international spirit been diminished or impaired? Has something happened to undermine the effectiveness of this unifying force in modern international law?

It will not come as a shock if my answer is that something very serious has happened. Major changes since World War I, and particularly since the Great Depression, have diminished the influence of the capitalist class with the result that international law has begun to lose its meaning. Since World War I, and especially since 1929, private organization of international economics has been increasingly sacrificed for collective organization under the centralized authority of the state.

A British economist, P. W. Martin, saw this as early as 1936, when he wrote, "The quasi-independent status of industry vis-à-vis the State has been replaced by a mixture of partnership and dependence which, whatever may be thought of it as a system, constitutes a totally new situation."[23] Martin's American counterpart, Eugene Staley, wrote in 1939: "The amount of central organization and conscious control in economic life is increasing. The movement in this direction, while extraordinarily rapid during the depression emergency . . . is a long-term phenomenon which antedates the depression and even the World War."[24]

As part of this phenomenon governmental powers and functions have multiplied at the expense of individual and private freedom. In recent years the state has increasingly controlled the exchange of goods, the flow of capital, the movement of the individual, and the exchange of ideas.

The rise of totalitarian states—Russia, Italy, Germany, and Japan—between the two world wars intensified that control, not only in the totalitarian states but also in the states menaced by them as well. Although World War II destroyed totalitarianism in Italy, Germany, and Japan, the tendencies toward state control have continued unabated. The Marxist threat is used as the chief explanation for these tendencies since World War II.

The communist states are crucial to this discussion for at least two reasons. First, because they represent the ultimate in state control of economic activities. Their collectivized economies require that international economic affairs be conducted in ways alien to those of other countries and unlike anything known even during the formative period of modern international law. Their economies, based on state planning, are administered from top to bottom by a state bureaucracy.

It follows that their international economic relations must coincide with a general economic plan if they are not to disrupt the domestic economy. Thus, the state must organize, direct, and actually transact foreign trade, as in fact it does. It is disquieting to know that the number of countries in which most external economic relations are under the direct control of the state is now greater than the number that existed prior to World War II.

Communist states also are important because of their ideology. The emergence of world communism has confronted international law with the new problem of trying to coordinate fundamentally different political, economic, and social systems into one international order: the problem of trying to find a place within the framework of the law for a legal and cultural structure alien to the general principles of internal order that have characterized the majority of states throughout the modern period. In other words, the emergence of world communism has shattered the capitalist content of the law.

Specialists debated the possibility of reconciling such extremes within a common system of international law at considerable length during the period between the two world wars. The English legal scholar Rudolf Schlesinger wrote that among legal experts of the western world it was a matter of heated debate "whether international law should be regarded as essentially bound to certain general principles of internal order which are characteristic of the majority of states, or interpreted as 'system-neutral' so that there is a place within its framework for any social structure known at the present time."[25]

As long as Marxism was in its infancy and the Soviet Union was weak, divided, and torn by internal strife, the whole question remained largely academic. Like Turkey, China, and other nonconformists before it, Russia could be made to obey, to toe the mark; in the 1920s and 1930s, a Russia on the make had little choice in the matter.

But even then Russian lawyers cautiously reminded the world that morality, law, and the state were "forms of bourgeois society" that communists might be compelled to use temporarily but that would eventually have to be abandoned because they could not be "filled with a socialist content."[26]

The following are random samples of Soviet opinion over the years on the subject of reconciling communism with modern international law. A statement from the Second Comintern Congress in 1920 read in part, "Under such conditions the Communists can have no confidence in bourgeois laws."[27] A quarter of a century later, not much had changed. "Like any other law," wrote Evgenii Korovin, one of Russia's leading legal experts, in 1946, "international law reflects the will of the ruling classes. The reality of international law, however, is not precluded by the fact that *for the time being* there are on the international stage bourgeois states as well as feudal and socialist states."[28]

More recently, in 1962, the Committee on Peaceful Co-Existence of the Soviet Association of International Law declared that "the principle of peaceful co-existence is a universally recognized principle of modern international law."[29] That might have been acceptable had "peaceful co-existence" not been defined two years later in the official history of the Communist party in these words: "Peaceful co-existence means competition in the economic and cultural spheres between countries of different social systems. This policy cannot lead to renunciation of the class struggle, to reconciliation of the socialist and bourgeois ideologies. It implies the development of the working class struggle for the triumph of socialist ideas."[30]

For more than half a century, the Soviet Union and other communist countries have worked within the international legal system rather than, as one writer has put it, "assaulting the system from without in the tradition of a revolutionary firebrand."[31] In the 1920s and 1930s the reason was simple: the Soviet Union was too weak to do otherwise. Since World War II, the Soviet Union has felt the pressure of new realities—great power status and the nuclear and space ages.

Soviet ideologists have labored to construct new myths to meet these new realities. Even so, Soviet scholars have been singularly unsuccessful in explaining how a single body of international law can apply equally to socialist and capitalist states. The finest legal minds in the Soviet Union have been no more successful in reconciling traditional Marxism with modern international law than have the legal experts in the western world. On the contrary, the persistent theme, stated or implied, is that only the ultimate triumph of socialism over capitalism will solve the dilemma by superseding the present capitalist-oriented international law with socialist law.

The trends toward state economic control at the international level noted earlier suddenly accelerated after the 1920s. With the world economy experiencing global depression, private enterprise, from an urgent sense of necessity, acquiesced to increasing state control, which brought the ascendancy of political considerations over private economic needs. In other words the post–World War I period found individuals appealing to their governments to use political power to rescue them from economic crisis. The governments responded, but with unexpected results.

Whether governmental intervention was good or not is irrelevant. Governmental intervention seriously weakened the integrity of what had once been an individualistic world economic system. That intervention implied the ultimate replacement of the traditional system by a state-planned and state-directed economic order. I contend that in the past fifty years or more the power of states all over the world has unhorsed the bourgeois capitalist class. Whatever may have been the faults of that class, it had the one virtue of unity. Traders and businessmen and all money makers desire the same things—order and amity. In this desire they are the bulwark for international law. States do not have such unity. States want advantage and seek it through some form of force, whereas businessmen seek advantage by bargaining.

The steady, irresistible spread of state control throughout economic life, both domestic and international, stems from powerful forces, greater even than wars or depressions, that have been gathering over a long period of time. The emphasis here has been placed on the influence of the New World discoveries on the growth and development of an economic system that imbued the national states with a capitalist point of view. If opening the New World played such a prominent part in the development of the capitalist economic system, it should follow that closing the New World frontier would, as Webb has pointed out, exert an equally important impact. On the consequences of the closing of the New World as a frontier, Webb's words are filled with foreboding:

Governments will tend to become stronger, using more compulsion in order to meet their obligations. There will be a tendency toward socialization as now exhibited in the United States and Great Britain or toward absolutism as exhibited by the fascist states and by Russia. The loose democracy belonged to a frontier stage of society. The individual will become relatively less important and will tend to lose his identity in a growing corporate life. Food and clothing should in the logic of affairs remain high in cost and go higher as population increases while land becomes relatively scarcer. The passing of free land should be registered by the passing of cheap food. Famine will continue to afflict overpopulated countries, and may return to Europe in spite of science. Capitalism of the nineteenth-century type will decline with the passing of the boom on which it was based. Its demand for area expansion cannot be met much longer.[32]

The New World, as a land frontier, closed about the turn of the century. By 1930, population had once again caught up to the available land. In other words, the ratio of people to land area resembled what it had been in the fifteenth century before the New World discoveries.[33]

The first decades of the twentieth century thus saw the end of what Webb described as "boom" conditions. It was also in this same period, between about 1900 and 1930, that the world system of private economic control began to run into serious trouble. There is, I believe, a relationship between these two conditions. As the boom conditions began to abate, hastened by the unusual and exhausting demands imposed upon the world economy by World War I, the power and the creative leadership of the bourgeoisie, upon whom the boom conditions had showered such bounties, likewise began to subside.

Let us assume that the world is, at the very least, in midstream of a great social and economic readjustment. Let us also suppose that the readjustment will continue for some time. How will this affect international law?

My hypothesis has been that modern international law evolved with the individual's quest for social and economic freedom. It was essentially a system of legal barriers to *prevent* the state from disturbing individual freedom. If the state is now usurping the role of the individual in world economic affairs, international law is being deprived of its original intent. To put it another way, modern international law was originally designed to *prevent* what has happened since the turn of the century. If this interpretation is correct, the present system has lost its raison d'être.

Significant differences exist between freedom of action for the individual and for the state. Freedom for the individual flourished only where legal guarantees existed; thus, in every state where men acquired freedom, there existed a bill of rights or its equivalent. Legislatures upheld it, courts defended it, society applauded it.

But freedom, remember, had been won from the state. International law was essentially another bill of rights—a means of preventing the state from intruding upon individual freedom on the international level, especially in economic affairs. Thus, one finds that during the nineteenth and early twentieth centuries efforts were made through law to control everything from patent rights to the caliber of armaments that might challenge that freedom.

The conditions necessary for state freedom are quite different from those necessary for individual freedom. From the international standpoint, freedom for the state implies the *absence* of legal restraints.

The state must be free to make decisions based on expediency or even force, without the handicap of legal barriers. This is the meaning of freedom for the state—a condition already achieved in some nations and that appears to be the trend in others. It is a situation—and this is the alarming part—that fitted states in the seventeenth century. The present historical conditions with which international law must deal are, in many ways, more nearly like those in Grotius's time than at the turn of this century.

In 1900, bourgeois capitalism was the dominant force providing society with its individualistic and creative style. Now, as in the time of Grotius, bourgeois capitalism is on the defensive; and, with each passing day, it finds itself subordinated still further to the will of the state. There is one significant difference. In Grotius's time the power of the bourgeois increased steadily at the expense of the state. The process now appears reversed, with the bourgeoisie steadily sacrificing power to national authority.

In 1947, Thorsten Kalijarvi, a regular legal consultant for many years to the Senate Foreign Relations Committee, who understood better than most what was happening, wrote that international law "is in need of modernization; it must be so changed that it will give prime consideration to the political aspects rather than the legalistic."[34] Kalijarvi was calling for a modernization of international law that would recognize the new and expanded political requirements of the state.

International law developed to meet a unique set of conditions, boom conditions, Webb called them. Since those conditions no longer exist, international law seems destined for some fundamental change. In short, modern international law is no longer modern, because the conditions that created it no longer exist. The challenge is to find some new force—the equivalent of the New World discoveries— through which to express international unity and a new spirit of the law before international law breaks down completely.

After the damage to international law inflicted by World War I, America's great legal scholar Roscoe Pound wrote this cautiously optimistic statement: "The conditions to which international law must be applied today are no more discouraging than those that immediately followed the Thirty Years' War. And we have the immeasurable advantage that we may build upon the permanent achievements of the classical international law. Our chief need is a man with that combination of mastery of the existing legal materials, philosophical vision and juristic faith which enabled the founder of international law [Hugo Grotius] to set it up almost at one stroke."[35]

The world is still awaiting the new Grotius of whom Professor Pound wrote so eloquently after World War I. But one thing is certain. The starting point for the new Grotius and his system of law must be the sociopolitical situation of our time in which the state is supplanting the individual as the prime mover in society.

"These are revolutionary times," wrote Professor Richard Erickson in his recent book, *International Law and the Revolutionary State*, published in 1972. "The traditional 'law of nations,' " he continued, "is western in origin, and, consequently, has been challenged in rising crescendo since World War I by the growth of communism and by the multiplication of newly independent states." Contemporary international law is meeting challenges, according to Erickson, "unparalleled since the days of Grotius."[36] He concluded that we are in a period of transition "from a system of international law of the Western European and North American family of Christian nations to a universal law of the world community."[37]

Erickson's book is interesting, even exciting, but he has missed the mark. Before the transition of which he writes can succeed, a transition further complicated by man's reach into space, another ingredient must be added.

The missing ingredient is the basis for cohesion, an equivalent to the unity from which sprang the spirit of the law provided at an earlier time by the might of Rome, later by the moral imperative of the Roman Catholic church, and, since Grotius's time, by the New World discoveries that produced an interrelated and interdependent bourgeois capitalist society.

This discourse began with a discussion of space law, and that is where it will also end. We need not be lulled by the apparent progress in this field. Thus far, the enormously expensive investment in space has been relatively fruitless except for scientific knowledge, which is inherently sharable. If celestial bodies remain, as they are now, economically unattainable, or if they eventually prove economically unprofitable, then the legal conflicts in space will probably be minimal. But, whether man is destined to continue in space or remain earthbound, a new unity and a new spirit of the law will be necessary before international law can once again be modern.

NOTES

1. Oscar Schachter, "Who Owns the Universe?" *Collier's*, March 22, 1952, p. 36.

2. Adlai Stevenson, address to the United Nations, December 4, 1961, reprinted in *Department of State Bulletin* 46 (1962): 180–185.

3. Albert Gore, quoted in E. W. Haughney, "Criminal Responsibility in Outer Space," in *Proceedings of the Conference on Space Science and Space Law*, University of Oklahoma, June 18–20, 1963, ed. M. D. Schwartz (Hackensack, N.J., 1963), pp. 146–150.

4. Martin Menter, "Formulation of Space Law," in *Proceedings of the Sixth Colloquium on the Law of Outer Space*, ed. Andrew Haley (Washington, D.C.: International Astronautical Federation, 1964), p. 2.

5. *New York Times*, September 23, 1960, text of speech by Dwight D. Eisenhower, p. 18.

6. John F. Kennedy, quoted in Edwin Diamond, "That Moon Trip: Debate Sharpens," *New York Times Magazine*, July 28, 1963, pp. 10, 23, 25.

7. Lyndon B. Johnson, quoted in S. Houston Lay and Howard J. Taubenfeld, *The Law Relating to Activities of Man in Space* (Chicago: University of Chicago Press, 1970), p. 29.

8. Edwin Maxey, *International Law with Illustrative Cases* (St. Louis: F. H. Thomas Law Book Co., 1906), p. 1.

9. G. J. van der Mandere, "Grotius and International Society of Today," *American Political Science Review* 19 (1925): 805.

10. James Brown Scott, *The Spanish Conception of International Law and of Sanctions* (Washington, D.C.: Carnegie Endowment for International Peace, 1934), p. 2.

11. James Leslie Brierly, *The Law of Nations* (London: Oxford University Press, 1942), p. 8.

12. Sir Robert Phillimore, *Commentaries upon International Law*,

3d ed. (London: Hodges, Foster and Co., 1879), 1, xxxvi.

13. Pasquale Fiore, *International Law Codified and Its Legal Sanction* (New York: Baker, Voorhis and Co., 1918), p. 6.

14. John Westlake, *Chapters on the Principles of International Law* (Cambridge: At the University Press, 1894), p. 50.

15. David Jayne Hill, quoted in Maxey, *International Law with Illustrative Cases*, p. 7 n. 1.

16. Julius Ludwig Goebel, *The Struggle for the Falkland Islands* (New Haven: Yale University Press, 1927), p. xi.

17. Walter Prescott Webb, *The Great Frontier* (Austin: University of Texas Press, 1964), pp. 13–28.

18. Ibid., p. 413.

19. Gerhart Niemeyer, *Law without Force* (Princeton: Princeton University Press, 1941), p. 59.

20. Ferdinand Schevil, "Can Our Civilization Achieve a More Stable World Order?" in *The Foundations of a More Stable World Order*, ed. Walter Herman Carl Laves (Chicago: University of Chicago Press, 1941), p. 17.

21. James Burnham, *The Managerial Revolution* (New York: John Day Co., 1941), p. 69.

22. Webb, *The Great Frontier*, p. 174.

23. P. W. Martin, "The Present Status of Economic Planning: An International Survey of Governmental Economic Intervention," *International Labour Review* 33 (May 1936): 631.

24. Eugene Staley, *World Economy in Transition* (New York: Council on Foreign Relations, 1939), p. 158.

25. Rudolf Schlesinger, *Soviet Legal Theory* (London: Routledge and Kegan Paul, 1951), p. 273.

26. Ibid., p. 156.

27. Second Comintern Congress, quoted in Ronald Christensen, *Soviet Views on Space: A Comparative and Critical Analysis*, Space Flight Report to the Nation, American Rocket Society (October 1961), p. 6.

28. Evgenii A. Korovin, *Bolshevik* (Moscow, 1946), p. 25 (italics are mine).

29. *Committee on Peaceful Co-Existence of the Soviet Association of International Law*, quoted in Leon Lipson, "Peaceful Co-Existence," in *Soviet Impact on International Law*, ed. Hans Baade (Dobbs Ferry,

N.Y.: Oceana Publications, 1965), p. 27.

30. *The History of the Communist Party of the Soviet Union* (Moscow: Foreign Languages Publishing House, 1964), p. 97.

31. Richard J. Erickson, *International Law and the Revolutionary State* (Dobbs Ferry, N.Y.: Oceana Publications, 1972), p. 165.

32. Webb, *The Great Frontier*, p. 415.

33. Ibid., p. 18.

34. Thorsten V. Kalijarvi, "International Law," in *Modern World Politics* (New York: Thomas Y. Crowell Co., 1947), p. 108.

35. Roscoe Pound, "Philosophical Theory and International Law," in *Bibliotheca Visseriana* (Leyden: E. J. Brill, 1923), 1, 108.

36. Erickson, *International Law and the Revolutionary State*, p. ix.

37. Ibid.

Webb
the
Schoolteacher

Walter Rundell, Jr.

Walter Prescott Webb stood at the pinnacle of his career in 1958. He
was president of the American Historical Association, the highest
honor his profession could bestow, and he had been awarded an hon-
orary doctorate by the University of Chicago. Three years earlier the
Mississippi Valley Historical Association had named him its president.
Thus, by 1958 he had become one of the rare historians to head the
two major learned societies in the discipline. The road to such eminence had been uncertain, if filled with high adventure. Before 1958
probably 90 percent of the seventy AHA presidents had received their
training and had taught at East Coast universities. Most had doubtless followed an unbroken progression from secondary school through

college and graduate school. Webb arrived at a position of leadership in the profession from a totally different direction. His intellectual journey started along the dusty country roads of West Texas that led to Throckmorton and Cisco, then to Austin, away to Beeville, San Marcos, Cuero, San Antonio, and back to Austin. Surely a most unusual circuit for one who became a master of his craft.

But that mastery is not the focus of this essay. Rather, it examines the beginnings of Webb's professional career in an effort to discern those elements in his experiences as a schoolteacher that foreshadowed or contributed to his intellectual maturation.

In his earliest autobiographical essay, "The Chain," written in November 1909 during his initial term at the University of Texas, Webb claimed that he "early became a lover of books." The volumes available to him in his father's modest library and in his one-room country school were a miscellaneous collection. But he read them and yearned for more. "Through this reading," Webb recalled, "there came a message of a different life, and I became ambitious and restless. I had experienced only the hard side of farm life and had come to hate the farm, the stumps, the bony horses, and the lean squealing pigs." Because of his family's poverty, he had to drop out of school for two years and then in the following two could go only "on the rare occasions when there was no work to be done." When he complained about not attending high school, his father said that he wanted Walter to receive an education, but that there was no money to send him.

Doing what he could to facilitate his son's education, Casner P. Webb moved from rural Stephens County into nearby Ranger so that Walter could enroll in high school in the fall of 1905. By building fires and sweeping floors, Walter earned money for his expenses, and, after passing the examination for a second-grade teaching certificate, he began teaching in a one-room rural school at Center Point in the summer of 1906. By saving money from teaching during that summer and winter, he could spend another year in high school. In the spring of 1908, he graduated and qualified for a first-grade certificate. Turning his sights toward earning money for college, he taught a year in the rural school at Merriman.[1]

Meanwhile, Webb had corresponded for five years with William E. Hinds, the unseen benefactor from Brooklyn whose funds helped Webb through his undergraduate years. Webb first came to Hinds's attention when, in 1904, *The Sunny South,* an Atlanta weekly, published Webb's letter to the editor. In this letter, Webb told his desire for an education and explained his lack of funds. Hinds responded by sending him books, magazine subscriptions, and, later, money. In addition to furnishing such journals as *Twentieth Century Review, American Boy, National Magazine, McClure's, Current Literature, Review of Reviews,* and *Success,* Hinds offered sage advice. Obviously steeped in the Protestant ethic, Hinds urged Webb to work hard, take a positive view of life, and think of success.[2] He counseled Webb to read the best works of fiction—Scott, Dickens, Thackeray, George Eliot, Hawthorne, Cooper, and Irving—and to practice descriptive writing. In one letter written when he was seventeen, Webb evidently discussed socialism in a favorable context, for Hinds responded that he supposed Webb had become "a full fledged Socialist."[3]

Hinds's letters also contained extensive descriptions of his activities and observations in New York City. He hoped to instruct not only Webb but also his students with accounts of the Brooklyn Academy of Music and excursions into Williamsburgh (the Jewish section of Brooklyn), the Bowery, and Chinatown. At the end of a long letter he appended the note: "Glad to have you read anything in my letter to your scholars (that you wish)." No doubt Webb's students in Merriman in the spring of 1909 learned from this first-hand account about the Williamsburgh fish market—open day and night, Jews with long whiskers, and the subway. Hinds also sent Webb and his students a four-volume encyclopedia dictionary and a Lincoln centennial series from the *New York Times.*[4]

The five-year correspondence between Webb and Hinds had convinced the latter that an investment in Webb's higher education was sound. In August 1909, before Webb entered the University of Texas, Hinds instructed Webb to let him know how much money he needed. During his university years, Webb received loans regularly from Hinds. Both parties kept strict account of these debts, and Webb made payments on the notes when he could. Hinds was not indulgent, for he reminded Webb to establish and maintain a repayment schedule and not become burdened with debt. He also suggested that Webb earn some portion of his expenses by working at the university. Throughout, Hinds declared that he was helping Webb help himself —that Webb must be prepared for future opportunities.[5]

Webb had to intersperse practical experience with his university education. For the fall term of 1911 he took charge of the Throckmorton rural high school. According to his employers, "He taught a successful school and gave entire satisfaction. Mr. Webb left of his own accord and against the wishes of the trustees and community to pursue his studies at the State University."[6] The spring term of 1912 found him teaching at the Britton Training School in Cisco. According to the president of that institution, Webb rendered dependable and capable service and possessed "those characteristics of loyalty that make one desire to bind him in closer ties."[7] The school superintendent in Rochester described Webb as a "live school man" who could be rehired at the schools where he had taught. Webb's "liveliness" encompassed commanding the attention and respect of students, being systematic in his work, and acting in harmony with every school interest. He was courteous yet firm toward students.[8]

This superintendent, Paul R. Crowley, had been one of Webb's closest boyhood friends in rural Stephens County. During Webb's undergraduate days, Crowley proved his friendship by frequently lending him money without interest to meet school expenses.[9] Having gotten an earlier professional start than Webb, he understood the political intricacies of school appointments in rural and small-town Texas. Knowing the right trustees mattered a great deal, and teachers were hired on the basis of individual pull. Once, when angling for the superintendency in Post City, Crowley confided that, if he got the job, he intended appointing Webb principal.[10]

Another school principal had reason to want Webb on his staff in Scranton: he planned to run for the county superintendency in Stephens County and figured that, as Webb's employer, he would have "a better stand-in with your folks." He was disappointed that Webb turned down an $80-per-month job at the Scranton Academy for more money elsewhere.[11]

During the 1913 spring semester at the University of Texas, Webb knew that for economic reasons he must teach during the following academic year. In addition to casting his net in Scranton, he applied to Jacksboro, Lubbock, and Beeville, all of which offered him jobs. From the $80-per-month low at the Scranton Academy, a coeducational boarding school, the offers ranged to $90 per month at Lubbock and $100 per month at Jacksboro and Beeville. The Jacksboro post was a principalship, whereas that in Beeville was teaching high school history. Webb accepted the latter, much to his mother's delight. She was "proud to hear of the good salary" and thought life in the coastal plain of South Texas would be "much more pleasant . . . than out West."[12]

His first impression of Beeville in August 1913 was that the town seemed settled and conservative in its habits and that personal affairs were everybody's business.[13] The next month, he called Beeville "a town with a personality—striving for prominence and publicity. . . . Though it has never dared utter the word 'city,' still that is the one word it craves to pronounce. The streets are all named, though no one knows the names. They are putting electric lights on the streets, numbers on the houses, departments in the school, collars on the dogs, and solos in the churches."[14] Webb believed that an annual ball epitomized Beeville's pretentiousness. Citizens gladly indebted themselves "to shine for four or five hours," and they employed a dancing master to teach "the tango and all its companion vagaries to the youth of Beeville." Webb noted sadly that each schoolgirl taking up the tango failed in her classwork.[15]

Webb had his hands full at the A. C. Jones High School in Beeville. He not only taught history and algebra but also had plenty of extracurricular responsibilities. He commented frequently on the unwillingness of some students to work and on the burden of grading examination papers. His remarks revealed modest expectations of human nature, yet they also showed compassion for those making honest efforts. He found that no loafers passed his exams but that some who worked also failed. Concerning the latter, he said: "But I shall see that the faithful do not suffer. Their class work will pull them over."[16] At the end of the semester, Webb's exams made it easy on students— as well as himself. He explained that he computed grades chiefly from the class record, so it was "useless to give long tests, especially at the last."[17] Since seniors were preoccupied with graduation activities, he did not insist on their continued work. Similarly, when other classes had covered the expected material, they could either review or do nothing. He exempted some students altogether.[18] Obviously, Webb was no martinet.

Students responded to Webb's understanding nature. Early in the fall he established excellent rapport with the boys by hiking and swimming with them, and they in turn crowned him a "king of good fellows." When they also tried to replace their Boy Scout leader with Webb, he smoothed the matter over by becoming assistant scoutmaster. He reported all the high school boys—ninety or one hundred—as members of the troop. "They are a wholesome set of kids, and I am looking forward with some pleasure to teaching them woodcraft, camp life, animal life and habits, path finding, pioneering, and scoutcraft in full so far as I am able. The Scout movement is a good thing and tends to develop the better parts of a boy's nature." Webb remained uncertain about the impact he had on his female students, claiming that he did not know much about girls, despite having grown up with three sisters. He took some pride in having overheard one student say that she had learned more history from him than ever before.[19]

One of the Beeville girls, who thought Webb a "wonderful" teacher with a fine disposition and a good sense of humor, commented on his classroom methods. Before each lesson he assigned the entire class a certain number of pages to read. After opening the discussion, he called on various members of the class to react to the topic on the basis of their reading; then he would analyze other aspects of the subject not found in the textbook. He established his reputation in Beeville so quickly that many boys who had dropped out of school came back because of him.[20]

Webb remembered most fondly having organized the high school literary society. The initial meeting reminded him of his own high school days, "so full of happiness, foolishness and conceit."[21] Each program featured someone from the town to talk to members, who took a lively interest in the unusually entertaining meetings. The extension department, as Webb called the Division of Extension, at the university prepared sets of lantern slides and lectures on such subjects as architecture, great paintings, and Luther Burbank's work.[22] For a meeting in early March 1914, Webb decided to present the literary society with an illustrated lecture from the extension department on great paintings. His activity as sponsor reflected the varied roles expected of the small-town schoolteacher. All preparations for the Saturday night meeting were left in his hands. He helped haul chairs and a piano, painted signs, wrote about half a publicity report the students had neglected to finish, conducted a rehearsal of the student program, arranged the stage for their program that night, and delivered his lantern-slide lecture. That day proved to be his "busiest and most strenuous" in a long time. One of the student performers at the literary society was a soprano "with a wonderful voice," Fay Gregory, whom Webb described as his favorite. She sang and gave two encores. Webb's lecture was so popular that the Beevillers requested him to repeat it in town, which he gladly did.[23]

Because of this success, Webb planned to use another lantern-slide lecture for the May meeting of the literary society. Despite having written twice and visited the extension department once to get the slides on architecture, Webb learned on the morning of the meeting that the slides would not arrive. With tickets sold, Webb had to explain the situation to the "bloodthirsty" audience, and he tried to appease them by returning half the admission price because the illustrated lecture comprised only part of the entertainment, and "we need the other half." He had planned some good musical selections—male quartets, duets, solos—and a comedy, plus a student parody on the faculty.[24] When the audience learned there would be no lecture on architecture, only half asked for the partial refund, "and those who did gained the contempt of all who knew about it." The faculty "take off" was the hit of the evening.[25]

Student skits constituted a chief form of entertainment at the Beeville high school. When the school's tennis team, coached by Webb, won the state championship in its Interscholastic League division in the spring of 1914, the school celebrated by staging a three-act farce on the performance of the tennis heroes in Austin. Girls represented the boys and a curly-haired boy portrayed the one female in the skit. Webb reported, "It was the cleverest thing I have seen."[26]

A teacher's reaction to any particular job is molded by the kinds of students, colleagues, and administrators he works with. In Beeville, Webb reacted favorably toward his students, though his bright September impression became tempered throughout the year. Initially, he found "as fine a set of young Americans as the average school affords. Barring a few 'bad ones' among the boys, and a few conscious beauties and would-be society belles among the young ladies, prospects flatter."[27] By midyear he diagnosed students as "prodigal of their time and opportunities . . . the very brightest students . . . are the ones who are going to fail. They positively and consistently refuse to work in any manner." With semester exams looming, a few intelligent ones worked harder in an effort to salvage their grades, and Webb wished them well.[28] When he returned from Austin with his tennis team in May, Webb discovered that two of his grown boys had used his absence as an excuse for fisticuffs in his classroom, which earned them an indefinite suspension. Webb was glad to be rid of one, but the other had been a very good student.[29]

At the end of the school year, Cora Lee and Fay Gregory entertained the teachers and twenty high school graduates in their home. Since Fay was Webb's favorite student, he looked forward to the occasion, except that he had been asked to serve as toastmaster. Without the least idea of what he would say, he entertained the Micawberish hope that something would turn up. For Webb, students like the Gregorys made teaching worthwhile.[30]

If Webb found satisfaction in working with students in Beeville, his reaction toward colleagues was not so positive. He may not have made much attempt to interact with them intellectually or socially because of his shyness or because he considered them so banal. On one occasion, when he could not escape the company of fellow teachers, he bemoaned that they were "a band of stereotyped individuals" who discussed only school matters.[31] On April 21, 1914, the high school teachers held a San Jacinto Day picnic. Webb's enjoyment of the occasion approximated Santa Anna's on the same day seventy-eight years earlier. "It was all a matter of small talk about things I hear every day. I managed to get a number of the party half angry, and things were not so dull after that."[32]

School administrators presented different problems. Webb considered the superintendent spineless and devoid of ideas. Unless public sentiment demanded changes, the superintendent had insufficient courage to initiate anything. He preferred to hide a defect than to eliminate it, and when a cheating case surfaced, with indisputable evidence, the man simply swept it under the rug. Webb stated: "It is disgusting to meet a man so hopelessly devoid of moral courage, and further it is damaging to the teachers who have to suffer for his incapacity. In every way except this one our superintendent is an excellent man."[33]

Beeville's high school principal apparently had no redeeming virtues as an administrator. When the superintendent discovered that

Webb planned to leave at the end of the year, he promptly offered him the principalship with a big raise, hoping to retain his services. The superintendent had told the principal he might be fired, but the latter had made no move to get another job. Webb called him "a pitiful old recluse. . . . I do not think I ever saw a man who was so incompetent to get through life as this old Latin scholar."[34]

Webb's teaching at Beeville was evaluated both locally and by the University of Texas visitor of schools. The superintendent obviously thought well of his work, as did outside observers. During the first week of classes in January 1914, the Austin representative visited Webb's classes and reported to the superintendent that Webb's efforts improved history teaching about 1,000 percent over the previous year. Modestly, Webb commented: "This is perhaps not saying much when one considers that the history work was not accepted by the University last year. With a 1,000 percent improvement, it should go through."[35]

The university was also interested in how papers were graded, as well as in classroom performance. From time to time, Webb had to designate a set of examination papers for university inspection. Those he marked with special care.[36] However exhilarating a favorable report from a classroom visitor, Webb termed the experience unpleasant at best. He particularly disliked an inspector with only a curious eye but lacking the mind to either appreciate or understand. "I flatter myself that I have one qualification as a teacher, and that is, I can make a curious visitor feel about as badly out of place as he really is."[37]

The life of the schoolteacher in small Texas towns encompassed more than classroom duties, grading papers, and relating to students, colleagues, and administrators. During the years he taught in Beeville, San Marcos, and Cuero, Webb found diversion and recreation in several ways. Many of these were defined by time and place; others showed Webb striving to enlarge his cultural horizons. From Beeville, he went deer hunting in Live Oak County with two of his schoolboys. He shot no deer, but he discovered talents as the chief cook of the expedition. After mixing several unheard-of dishes that tasted good, he was acclaimed a treasure by the boys.

Both touring and resident preachers interested Webb. He enjoyed talking with traveling evangelists who ate at his boarding house, such as "the famous" Sid Williams, who came to Beeville in November 1913. Webb knew that Williams had made it rather disagreeable for some of the boarders, but Webb still liked him.[38] Webb proved a fairly regular churchgoer and commented perceptively on theological issues raised by preachers of the various churches he attended but never joined.[39] A typical Texan, Webb enjoyed games of dominoes and forty-two. In Beeville he participated in the forty-two Presbyterian Saturday Night Club, where conversation sparkled with wit and was "profound with wisdom."[40] The local hotel furnished a place for regular domino games after supper.[41]

During the fall of 1914, while in San Marcos, Webb expanded his recreational horizons and became proficient at the card game of five hundred. There he also continued to play tennis frequently, as well as row on the river and hike in the scenic countryside. Once, in September, when he went out on a pier in the river, he reported that "the water looked so clear and cool and inviting, and my feet burned so from standing that I was induced to do a very boyish thing. I pulled off my shoes and swung my feet off into that river for about half an hour. It sure was fine."[42]

Plays and movies, as well as serious music, appealed to Webb. He attended all the traveling theatrical productions that came to town and displayed great appreciation for drama. He liked film comedies, although he saw nothing special about Mary Pickford. Before being diverted into a game of five hundred one night, he had planned to see the film *La Tosca*, based on the play that he had seen Sarah Bernhardt perform in Austin. Recordings of *Il Trovatore* and Anton Dvorak's "Humoresque" appealed to him greatly, and he commented on them repeatedly.[43]

In the 1913–1914 winter Webb became seriously interested in Texas folklore, and he awarded Beeville and, later, Cuero students credit for stories they brought to class.[44] As he and his students began systematic collecting, his enthusiasm was contagious. He felt that he was a pioneer in the field and marveled that the supply seemed inexhaustible, increasing, in fact, like "the heads of the dragon." One Sunday at the hotel where he ate, he found two cowboys with a plentiful store of songs. He persuaded them to go to his room, where he could transcribe the songs. Original western stories and legends fascinated him more than songs, and he visited individuals in their homes to record their lore. One tale from Beeville concerned a scorned and insignificant weakling cowboy who gained freedom and the respect of his fellows by killing his tormentor.[45]

Webb communicated his interest in folklore to his mentors at the University of Texas, and, because of the impression he made there as a creative and imaginative student, John A. Lomax of the Folklore Society of Texas invited him to give a paper at its fourth annual meeting in May 1914. This paper, "Folklore Fields of the Southwest,"[46] became Webb's first scholarly contribution as "Notes on Folk-lore of Texas," published in 1915 by the *Journal of American Folk-lore*, edited by the renowned Franz Boas of Columbia University. In the process of publishing this manuscript, Boas had to prompt Webb to return his proof,[47] which the Austin post office had not forwarded to Webb.[48] When the tyro Webb sent Boas a check for one dollar, asking for some copies of the journal, Boas returned the check, informing Webb that he would receive fifty reprints free.[49] Webb ingenuously expressed surprise that Boas knew his identity when he sent the check, for Webb did not mention his forthcoming article. Little did he understand that editors remember tardy authors! Webb noted that fifty reprints would swamp him. He could figure out how to dispose of twelve or fifteen, "but never fifty."[50]

Always on the lookout for folklore, Webb discovered a fine source at the Cuero picture show. The promoter of a wild-west film made in Uvalde came to the Cuero high school, asking Webb to announce the picture to his students. Webb learned in talking with him that he was "a pure cowboy" and asked if he knew any songs. After school Webb hurried to the theater to transcribe three long songs, consisting of more than thirty stanzas. With those, he could prepare a paper for the next Folklore Society meeting that would "measure up with the best of them."[51]

Webb spent most of his schoolteaching career as a bachelor. Shortly before he moved to Beeville, he had become acquainted with his next-door neighbor in Austin, Jane Oliphant. Although they must have seen each other frequently, Webb's reticence prevailed until they had been properly introduced. The T. H. Shelbys provided this opportunity at a watermelon party in the summer of 1913.[52] As soon as he arrived in Beeville, Webb began a voluminous correspondence with Jane Oliphant that lasted until their marriage. These letters constitute the best source of information on Webb's activities and thoughts from August 1913 until September 1916, because he wrote frequently, at length, and with considerable style. He loved to write and receive letters, and historians can be thankful that Mrs. Webb understood their value and kept them all.

Almost from the beginning of their relationship, Webb was the ardent swain. For many months Jane found the correspondence pleasant but would not commit herself to any profession of affection. Only after he overwhelmed her with the intensity and purity of his devotion did she begin to acknowledge a reciprocal feeling. Because of the difference in their temperaments, they disagreed on important matters. As soon as they began to consider marriage, these disagreements loomed large. Webb assumed, for instance, that, if she loved him enough to marry him, there should be no question about her going where his work took him. But she seemed to think that Austin was the only place to live in Texas. Unquestionably, she had high aspirations for his career, and she possibly realized that Austin was where his talents could be cultivated and matured.[53] Webb always felt, however, that her reluctance to follow him resulted from a selfish unwillingness to give up her teaching at the state school for the deaf, as well as the very pleasant aspects of life in Austin.[54] She eventually did move to San Antonio as a bride but returned to Austin two years later to remain for the rest of her life, as did he. From the time Webb began his epistolary courtship, his love affair with "Jean," "Jane," or "Janey"—depending on his mood—preoccupied his life as a schoolteacher.

In May 1914 Webb knew he would not return to Beeville, for the University of Texas had awarded him a scholarship in institutional history for 1914–1915. He planned to study again under Professor Lindley M. Keasbey, the man who had most influenced his thinking, with a munificent stipend of $100 per year, plus remission of fees.[55] The more prestigious university fellowships paid $200 per year.[56]

An opportunity to earn more money at Southwest Texas Normal School forced Webb to forego the scholarship for the fall semester, and the university allowed him to assume it for the following spring.[57] Negotiations with the normal school in San Marcos opened with President C. E. Evans asking Webb to apply for an English instructorship. Webb gladly responded, saying he had had every composition course offered at the university, plus two in literature. Webb held high hopes for the post, for it would mean, among other things, that he would "never teach another day in the public schools." For him this would be a dream come true.[58] His only apprehension concerned the lack of a degree. Evans decided that Webb was not destined to become an English teacher but offered him the job of registrar and bookkeeper for the autumn semester, pending the return of the regular occupant of those posts. In addition, Webb taught a freshman course in education. This course and the registrar's duties were undemanding, but Webb wrestled with the books during his four months in San Marcos. He had no training in bookkeeping, and the system proved both elaborate and arcane; by the time he left, however, he had overcome a great backlog and had balanced the books.[59]

Webb discovered that normal school students were much more serious and studious than those at the university and the high schools where he had taught. Most, he surmised, "are fortunate enough not to be rich and know, therefore, why they are here." The girls outnumbered the boys three-to-one, so the normal school boasted little "varsity" spirit. Webb applauded the teachers' close personal contact with students and declared that "one finds among them much more red blood and humanity than among those cowardly freshman teachers at Austin."[60] Without any discipline problems, and with students "eager and hungrily attentive," Webb found his teaching conditions ideal.[61] In addition to his education class, Webb sometimes "heard" classes for the head of the history department, the recitation method still being in vogue.[62] After the exhilaration of teaching at the normal school, Webb could not bear the idea of returning to the public schools.[63]

A highlight of that November was the annual meeting of the Texas State Teachers Association in San Antonio. Webb anticipated going so that he could meet "all the better teachers in the state." The trip exceeded his expectations. "Dr. Battle spoke to me and actually laughed—you know he usually smiles a smile that is cold and damp like the mirth of a fish. Benny said 'Howdy, Webb.' Mr. Lomax . . . said he wanted me to . . . come see him. . . . My mixing up with all those highbrows made my head swell up until it hurt all the next day."[64] At the meeting Webb heard a speaker expostulate on teaching as a noble but underpaid profession. These clichés soothed Webb "just like the flapping of a shutter in the north wind at about 1:30 in the morning."[65] Throughout his career, he refused to be patronized by anyone extolling the virtue of the teaching profession.[66]

Webb returned to the university to earn his B.A. degree at the end of the 1915 spring semester. He soon learned that the post of principal and history teacher of the San Marcos high school was open and applied for it. A. W. Birdwell, head of the history department at the normal school, urged him to be a candidate, informing him that the job paid about $1,400 a year. Webb's application stated that "my whole preparation has been made with the purpose of becoming a school man. I am not making school work a means to an end, but an end in itself."[67] In view of his earlier hope never to have to teach another day in public schools, Webb's eagerness for the San Marcos position indicated that economic need had tempered ambition. The San Marcos job did not materialize, but a similar one in Cuero did at $1,200 a year.[68]

Shortly after Webb arrived in town, Cuero put on a display that convinced him the town had possibilities. His second day there a fistfight erupted in front of the Butler Hotel, where he had registered, and that night at a Negro revival the fire and brimstone gave way to a shooting scrape.[69] Yes, Cuero was a "splendid little town," with "plenty of churches and saloons." This was Webb's pronouncement after having seen the town—"by walking around the block." In a more serious vein, he commented that Cuero was clean and well kept, with many pretty houses and lawns—the best town he had seen south of San Antonio, except Corpus Christi.[70] He took a room at the Breeden house that cost $10 per month and learned that meals at the Baker boarding house would run to $20 a month, which he considered rather expensive.[71]

No sooner had he gotten settled than he had to spend a few days in nearby Yorktown at a school institute. School districts often held such meetings, before opening in the fall, to bring teachers up to date on methods of instruction. When Webb taught in San Marcos, he had taken his education class to a local institute to dispel any fears they may have entertained about the intellectual demands of such gatherings.[72] The Yorktown conclave was typically female, with about eighty women and twenty men. One lecture on teaching Scott's "Lady of the Lake" so engrossed Webb that he thought of Janey throughout. Because she told him she found institutes interesting, he wondered if a recent fever had affected her mind.[73]

Besides his work as principal of the Cuero high school, Webb taught six recitations in four different history courses. Because his eight teachers were strong, he thought his duties as principal would be light, but this assumption proved wrong.[74] The first duty involved the school's opening ceremonies on September 13. He expressed a mild dread about making a maiden speech to expectant students, teachers, trustees, and town notables. But the problem did not worry him excessively, for he turned his hand to preparing his remarks after ten o'clock the night before. The "4⅞'s minute" speech proved a success, chiefly because he referred to the football team. The superintendent seemed highly pleased and Webb got a big ovation. He had hit the ground running in Cuero.[75]

During his year at Cuero, Webb's duties as principal and teacher were heavy, especially since the older teachers had been able to unload some of their classes on him as the new man. The superintendent, A. S. Bush, whom Webb admired greatly, appreciated Webb's accepting his assignment without grumbling and assured him of a lighter schedule the following year.[76] As principal, Webb participated in all phases of the school. Toward the beginning of the year, he had to "inflict the corporal on two young Americans." As the year progressed, his responsibilities included producing the senior play, paying school bills, attending teachers' meetings and the PTA, eating lunches prepared by domestic-education girls, traveling with athletic squads, coaching baseball, marching in a George Washington's Birthday procession, and producing a minstrel show to raise money for a yearbook.[77] But Webb complained little. In fact, he described his work with teachers and parents most favorably. He thought that teachers' meetings were the only way to ensure a unified approach to high school education, and he expected that the PTA would enable the school to enlist cooperation from the homes.[78] Among his onerous chores was recording all student grades in the school's permanent record, after, of course, he had figured and recorded grades for his six history classes. "Teaching," Webb said, "is little short of pure drudgery, especially when it comes to the paper grading and bookkeeping part of it."[79]

Nevertheless, Webb refused to be subdued by the mechanics of his work. In Cuero he displayed imagination and originality in the class-room—a willingness to essay something different and venturesome that later characterized his books. Classes were only in their second week when he decided he would adapt Dr. Keasbey's problem method of teaching to his tenth-grade English history class. He chose that class because it had just a dozen students, and he feared that the problem method would not work in his large eleventh-grade American history class. Webb thought Dr. Keasbey would be pleased to know of this innovation—that students would approach historical phenomena through reasoning about their various interrelating aspects and by reaching conclusions for themselves, based on given data.[80] This method differed sharply from the rote memory required in standard recitation sections. (In the 1960s the problem method gained great vogue in the schools as something new, being termed the discovery or inductive method of learning.) Webb was pleased with this pioneering effort and planned to extend it to American history the following year. He even thought about someday writing a doctoral dissertation on this teaching innovation. He had "visions of changing the method of teaching history in the Texas high schools, state adopted texts, royalties, and other such wild and fanciful fool notions. At any rate . . . I am following my star and living my own life, and I am going to live it according to my light, no matter where it may lead."[81] This 1915 declaration could have been his epitaph.

Less than a month before Webb wrote the above comments, a series of events had been set in motion that influenced and shaped the remainder of his life. A. W. Birdwell, his San Marcos roommate whose classes he had taught at the normal school, invited him to deliver a paper for the history section of the Texas State Teachers Association meeting in Corpus Christi in late November 1915.[82] Having initiated his classroom experiment with the problem method, Webb decided to devote the paper to that topic. Since Birdwell suggested the topic of Webb's paper before Webb announced his decision to introduce the problem method into his class, possibly Birdwell deserves credit for sparking Webb's imagination.[83] The paper's title would be "Increasing the Functional Value of History by the Problem Method of Presentation."[84]

Considering the importance of this paper to Webb's life as a scholar, one is struck with his indecision over preparing it. The paper had to be ready for delivery on November 26, yet on October 24 he thought of giving it up because he had so little time to write it—having cogitated about it since September 14! Also, Janey refused to commit herself to being in Corpus Christi for the meeting, and he figured that, without her there, the paper would not be worth undertaking.[85] Despairing of a definite response, in early November he finally addressed himself to the task and developed a "working humor." For the two weeks remaining before the meeting, he devoted the hours of eight to eleven each evening to his writing. By November 22 it was finished and Webb hired a typist for the final draft. He admired the final product and predicted that Birdwell, Dr. Frederic Duncalf of the university history department, and some others would be immensely pleased.[86]

The reception of the paper encouraged Webb. Among those impressed, as Webb foresaw, was Dr. Duncalf, a fellow panelist.[87] After the favorable response, Webb decided to submit it for publication, and the *History Teacher's Magazine* printed the article in May 1916.[88] Dr. Duncalf considered the paper so original and imaginative that, when the University of Texas had a position for someone to train history teachers for the schools, he recommended Webb, who finally received the appointment.[89] All along the way Webb had made the most of his opportunities, impressing critical observers with his ideas and performance. As a result, he got the big break that determined his illustrious career.

Even before his call to Austin, Webb gained significant recognition for the paper. A. W. Birdwell, currently enrolled at George Peabody College, was so enthusiastic about Webb's essay that he shared it with a professor. Together they followed its suggestions for teaching ancient history in the Peabody demonstration school.[90] When Webb enrolled for graduate courses at the University of Wisconsin in the summer of 1916, he discovered a woman in the library reading his piece. Overwhelmed with pride in communicating with some unknown person, he was equally curious to know the reader's reaction. He slipped a message across the table: "I note that you have been reading the article 'The Problem Method of Presentation.' What is your opinion of it as set forth in the article?" Her response: "Haven't entirely finished it as yet, but think it most interesting—and practical —if one has the sources." Webb scribbled: "I am glad you like it. I happen to be the writer." The woman also delighted Webb with the information that her professor had assigned the article to her entire class in history teaching.[91] Janey responded to this news ecstatically and prophetically. She knew the article would be instrumental in his future. "The first thing you know you will be offered a place in some university."[92]

As a serious and sensitive teacher, Webb was naturally concerned with the effectiveness of his work and his students' reaction to him. In Cuero, as in Beeville, student response to his teaching and personality gratified him. When Webb went to school the morning after Hallowe'en, he got a tangible demonstration of student affection. Hobgoblins had scrawled on the school bulletin board, "Mr. Webb and Mr. Barkley are our two best teachers," and on Webb's blackboard, this inscription, "Mr. Webb is our friend; we won't bother him." Elsewhere in the school all fire hoses were down, the superintendent had a beer keg in his office, and other rooms had been ransacked.[93]

As the principal, Webb was responsible for the overall operation of the high school, which inevitably involved him in the athletic program. Whether his interest was innate or feigned, he convinced students of his sincerity. After a 27-to-0 victory over Victoria, the football team visited Webb's home to give him a rousing fifteen rahs. He took special pride in Cuero's 21-to-0 win against Beeville, the ancient rival. All the Beeville squad had been his students two years earlier. After the game, Webb—always the teacher—arranged for both teams to hear Dr. Southwick, a dramatist, recite from *King Lear*. Later a wealthy Cueroite treated them to an oyster supper, which they may have enjoyed more. In any event, "the boys all went away talking about the good time they had."[94] On another night a band of spirited high school boys gathered at his gate and gave several yells for him. When he extended to them the hospitality of his limited quarters, they tramped upstairs to his room. Having nothing for them to eat, he "gave them all the hydrant water they could drink and sent them on their way rejoicing."[95]

Students indicated their esteem and appreciation in other ways. One boy made a typewriter table in woodworking class for Webb.[96] A dropout, whom Webb had put on the folklore trail while a student, continued to send material. He thanked Webb for his "many, many favors" and considerate treatment.[97] The artist "Buck" Schiwetz, taught by Webb in Cuero, commented on Webb's affection for his students: "He was very knowledgeable, patient, and knew how to communicate. . . . He was a far cry from the coterie of rather austere, I'd say colorless fellow instructors."[98]

Doubtless Webb took great satisfaction in the success of his teaching at Cuero and the warm student response. Yet the winter and spring of 1916 were a troubled time for him. Financial pressures clouded his future and strengthened an earlier resolve to improve his situation by moving to a more lucrative post or by leaving teaching altogether. Ambition always played a large part with Webb, and he constantly looked for a way to advance as an educator. When rumors circulated in the summer of 1915 about the creation of three new normal schools in Texas, Webb laid the groundwork with an Eastland County friend to secure an appointment in the one proposed for that region. Those plans collapsed when the normal school regents opposed expansion.[99] Early that autumn, Webb dreamed of returning to Beeville as superintendent. When it appeared that A. S. Bush, his Cuero boss, planned to leave, Webb was sure he would have Bush's support as his replacement.[100]

Soon Webb's thoughts turned toward a school job in Austin or San Antonio, where nondegree teachers were being replaced with those having degrees. With his new B.A. and a year's experience as principal, Webb could now qualify for a place in a large system. Simultaneous with these wishes, he thought more about teaching in a normal school, even if it meant relocating in the Pacific Northwest. T. H. Shelby counseled him that, if he wanted to take the normal school route, he should do graduate work at Columbia, for the big men in pedagogy were there. Somehow, prospects seemed more concrete nearer home—in San Antonio. Webb's landlord, R. P. Breeden, a close friend of the president of the San Antonio school board, promised to speak to him about Webb.[101] Breeden's influence had a good effect, for the president spoke to Superintendent Charles S. Meek, who met Webb and was sufficiently impressed to offer him a job at San Antonio's Main Avenue High School. Since the salary was the same as in Cuero, Webb's acceptance of the new post testified to his eagerness to meet the challenge of teaching in the city as well as his desire to live in a place that would please Janey, as he knew Cuero would not. He announced to her that he would not leave the San Antonio system so long as he stayed in the public schools.[102] Of his many emphatic pronouncements, that one came true.

Concurrent with Webb's angling for a better school position was his conflicting desire to leave teaching altogether. Behind both drives was the need for more money. He had spent all his life scraping to get by and had secured his university education only by becoming indebted. William E. Hinds had loaned Webb considerable sums, and Paul Crowley had provided smaller amounts. Webb repaid as he could, but for three years after Hinds's death he was willing to let that debt rock along, since no one called for repayment. Then, in September 1915, the lawyer handling Hinds's estate began to press Webb for settlement. Webb wrote Hinds's sister Ida, who expressed genuine sympathy with his situation. In March she loaned him the $303 that enabled him to pay off her brother's notes. She did not press for quick repayment, but by April 1917 she suggested firmly that he should have the entire debt retired within six months.[103]

Pressure for repaying the Hinds debt clouded Webb's entire year in Cuero. In the winter of 1916 he pipe-dreamed about two business ventures that would gain him financial independence so that he could pay off his debts and quit teaching. The first was a brokerage venture for selling groceries, fruits, cottonseed, and other farm products on commission. He quickly abandoned that scheme because he considered his potential partner unreliable, which he was—and Webb had known it from the beginning.[104] His mere entertaining the notion signified his desperation.

The next inspiration was a partnership for the manufacture and sale of toilet articles. With a local druggist making the toiletries and Webb as the front man on the road, they figured to make a 300 percent profit on their modest investment. Such reckoning was heady to one "sick of school work on starvation wages." He wrote Jane: "As long as I am alone I can get along. But for your sake I want money, money, money, and I am going to have it. The empty honor of teaching has lost its allurements for me." Within three weeks the dream of a fortune from toilet water had faded, although Webb insisted he had only postponed it.[105] Not being able to afford a two-dollar ticket to Griffith's *The Birth of a Nation* made Webb acutely aware of his plight.[106] Ultimately, his disillusion with the financial aspects of schoolteaching would lead him to abandon his calling. But that would be after two years of teaching in San Antonio, from 1916 to 1918.

There, Webb propounded the problem method of teaching history at the Main Avenue High School. He married Jane Oliphant in mid-September, shortly before classes began, and took her to San Antonio as his bride. This culmination of an ardent three-year courtship doubtless overshadowed his pedagogical activities. Yet, always sensitive to the way that classroom study related to the larger world of learning and ideas, Webb wrote an article entitled "How the War Has Influenced History Teaching in San Antonio High Schools." By giving them modern associations with historical phenomena, the war had quickened students' interest in history, as evidenced by a 79.8 percent enrollment increase. Webb pointed out that the Mission City furnished a compelling setting for the study of history, with its Spanish colonial heritage and current military activity.[107] Finally, the allurements of the big-city school—on a Cuero salary—wore thin. The old doubts about the worthiness and financial sacrifices of schoolteaching prevailed. Contributing to Webb's decision was his dispute with the superintendent over salary, as well as educational philosophy. The superintendent embraced the progressive notion that grades should encourage, rather than evaluate, students. Webb maintained a more traditional view but recognized that in this controversy Mr. Meek held the upper hand. After the end of the spring term in 1918, Webb gave up teaching to enter business as a bookkeeper for H. C. Rees, a downtown optometrist.[108] But he found the business world less exciting and rewarding than he had hoped, for he was still a teacher at heart.

In March 1918 the Department of History at the University of Texas negotiated to appoint Webb an instructor. Professors Frederic Duncalf and Eugene Barker made a written recommendation for Webb to the president, but without immediate effect.[109] Then, in the fall, Dr. Duncalf telephoned Webb at the Rees optometry shop to offer him the job of training history teachers.[110] Webb's call had come. He had parlayed his experience as a schoolteacher into the university post that would ultimately make him famous—and rich.[111]

The imaginativeness of Webb's high school teaching carried over into his forty-year career at the university. There he developed seminars around the ideas of his seminal books, *The Great Plains* and *The Great Frontier*. He and his graduate students jointly explored the intellectual dimensions of these topics, mutually enriching the others' knowledge. Webb devoted his presidential address to the Mississippi Valley Historical Association in 1955 to how the seminars had investigated and matured his ideas.[112] In teaching graduate students at the University of Texas he clearly demonstrated a willingness to break out of conventional pedagogical molds. The freedom of being a university professor had not fired his imagination, for he had displayed teaching creativeness in introducing the problem method in the Cuero high school, a much less likely place to inspire innovation in teaching. Obviously, the man, not the place, shaped his destiny.

In 1915 Webb had proclaimed that he intended to follow his own star, wherever it might lead. This statement, conveying the qualities of spunk, self-assurance, and creativeness—if not combativeness— seems prophetic. But for it to have come from a twenty-seven–year– old Cuero teacher, burdened with debts, was indeed remarkable. Webb's fame rests on the fulfillment of his promise, evidenced in *The Great Plains, The Texas Rangers, Divided We Stand,* and *The Great Frontier.* Of these four memorable books, only *The Texas Rangers* represents a conventional historical monograph, and it incorporated unconventional field research. This subject had originally been Webb's dissertation topic, but, as he investigated the Rangers' weaponry, he became aware of the impact of the Great Plains environment on the technology of the area. Fascinated with this insight, he put aside research on the Rangers to investigate the Great Plains. The 1931 book by that name became his dissertation, and in 1935 he published *The Texas Rangers.* Together they brought him fame and fortune. Paramount Pictures purchased movie rights to the latter, and the money he received provided the economic leverage that enabled him to invest successfully in Austin real estate.

Divided We Stand (1937) constituted further proof of Webb's independence of mind. He demonstrated how the North had kept the West and South in economic submission through patent monopolies, corporate manipulations, and the protective tariff. The summation of his life's thought, *The Great Frontier* (1952) portrayed vividly how the windfall of the world frontier had influenced and matured civilization and institutions. The volume was an eloquent culmination of a life and a mind shaped from the beginning by the geography and heritage of America's last frontier. Like all his other publications, this book provoked strong criticism. This was because Webb chose to work with ideas rather than merely to recount facts. By dealing with grand concepts, Webb deeply enriched historical thought.[113] Those qualities of his success as a historian—imagination, creativeness, independence of mind, and belief in the soundness of his ideas—all evidenced themselves during his days as a schoolteacher.

NOTES

1. "The Chain," English 1: 11, University of Texas, November 5, 1909, C. B. Smith Collection of Walter Prescott Webb Papers, Texas State Archives, Austin (hereafter referred to as CBS-WPW). The location of the teaching jobs came from my interview with Webb's youngest sister, Mrs. Ima Wright, Austin, Tex., July 25, 1973. She was his student at Merriman.
2. William E. Hinds to Dear Junior, New York, N.Y., September 10, 1904; to My dear boy, January 31, 1909; to W. Prescott Webb, April 29, 1909, CBS-WPW.
3. Hinds to Dear Friend, New York, N.Y., December 25, 1905, CBS-WPW.
4. Hinds to My dear boy, New York, N.Y., January 31, 1909; to Dear Friend, May 19, 1909, CBS-WPW.
5. Hinds to Dear Junior, New York, N.Y., August 8, 1909, June 26, 1911, CBS-WPW.
6. W. E. Parmenter and H. D. Killman to Whom It May Concern, Throckmorton, Tex., May 10, 1913 (copy), CBS-WPW. This letter does not specify that Webb was in Throckmorton for the 1911 fall term, but other evidence indicates that as the only likely time. He was out of the university in 1911–1912, and he taught in Cisco in the spring of 1912. Similarly, the dates of his earlier teaching cannot be established precisely from the information given in "The Chain," since that information is sometimes conflicting.
7. O. C. Britton to Whom It May Concern, Cisco, Tex., April 25, 1913 (copy), CBS-WPW.
8. Paul R. Crowley to Whom It May Concern, Rochester, Tex., May 12, 1913 (copy), CBS-WPW.
9. Crowley to Walt, Rochester, Tex., January 20, May 14, November 1, 1913, February 9, 1914, CBS-WPW.

10. Crowley to Walt, Rochester, Tex., January 20, 1913, CBS-WPW.
11. J. E. Temple Peters to Walt, Scranton, Tex., June 30, 1913, CBS-WPW. According to William A. Owens, the politics of rural schools had changed little by the 1920s, when he taught in several one-room East Texas schools (cf. *A Season of Weathering* [New York: Scribner's, 1973], pp. 52–53, 114–116, 174–175).
12. Peters to Walt, Scranton, Tex., June 30, 1913; James K. Wester, superintendent, Lubbock, Tex., high school, to Webb, June 6, 1913; L. Z. Timmons, superintendent of schools, Jacksboro, Tex., to Webb, June 5, 1913; W. E. Maderra, Beeville, Tex., to Webb, June 5, 1913; Mother to My Dear Son, Ranger, Tex., May 18, 1913, CBS-WPW.
13. Webb to Miss Janey Oliphant, Beeville, Tex., August 12, 1913, CBS-WPW.
14. Webb to Miss Janey Oliphant, Beeville, Tex., September 21, 1913, CBS-WPW.
15. Webb to My dearest Jean, Beeville, Tex., February 22, 1914, CBS-WPW.
16. Webb to My dearest Friend, Beeville, Tex., February 1, 1914, CBS-WPW.
17. Webb to My dear Jean, Beeville, Tex., May 28, 1914, CBS-WPW.
18. Webb to My dear Jean, Beeville, Tex., May 17, 25, 1914, CBS-WPW.
19. Webb to My dear Friend, The Bee City, Tex., October 1, 1913, CBS-WPW.
20. Fay Gregory to the author, Austin, Tex., September 23, 1974.
21. Webb to My dear Friend, Beeville, Tex., December 6, 1913, CBS-WPW.
22. Webb to My dearest Friend, Beeville, Tex., February 1, 1914, CBS-WPW.
23. Webb to My dear Jean, Beeville, Tex., March 9, 1914, CBS-WPW.
24. Webb to My dear Jane, Beeville, Tex., May 15, 1914, CBS-WPW.
25. Webb to My dear Jean, Beeville, Tex., May 17, 1914, CBS-WPW.
26. Webb to My dearest Jean, Beeville, Tex., May 9, 1914, CBS-WPW.
27. Webb to Miss Janey Oliphant, Beeville, Tex., September 21, 1913, CBS-WPW.
28. Webb to Miss Janey Oliphant, Beeville, Tex., January 11, 1914, CBS-WPW.
29. Webb to My dear Jean, Beeville, Tex., May 4, 1914, CBS-WPW.

30. Webb to My dear Jean, Beeville, Tex., May 30, 1914, CBS-WPW.

31. Webb to My dear Jean, Beeville, Tex., April 20, 1914, CBS-WPW.

32. Webb to My dear Jean, Beeville, Tex., April 21, 1914, CBS-WPW.

33. Webb to My dear Jean, Beeville, Tex., January 18, 1914, CBS-WPW.

34. Webb to My dear Jean, Beeville, Tex., May 17, 1914, CBS-WPW.

35. Webb to Miss Janey Oliphant, Beeville, Tex., January 11, 1914, CBS-WPW.

36. Webb to My dear Jean, Beeville, Tex., March 9, 1914, CBS-WPW.

37. Webb to My dear Jean, Beeville, Tex., February 14, 1914, CBS-WPW.

38. Webb to My dear Friend, Beeville, Tex., November 13, 1913, CBS-WPW.

39. Webb to My dearest Sweetheart Jean, Cuero, Tex., October 2, 1915, CBS-WPW.

40. Webb to Miss Janey Oliphant, Beeville, Tex., January 11, 1914, CBS-WPW.

41. Webb to My dear Jean, Beeville, Tex., April 21, 1914, CBS-WPW.

42.Webb to My dear Jean, San Marcos, Tex., September 22, 21, October 1, November 1, 22, 1914, CBS-WPW.

43. Webb to My dear Jean, Beeville, Tex., April 29, 1914; to My dearest Jean, San Marcos, Tex., October 11, 1914; to My dearest Sweetheart Jean, Cuero, Tex., October 2, 1915; to My dear Janey, Cuero, Tex., February 10, 1916, CBS-WPW.

44. Webb to My dear Jean, Beeville, Tex., January 18, 1914; to My own dear Janey, Cuero, Tex., October 30, 1915, CBS-WPW.

45. Webb to My Dear Jean, Beeville, Tex., February 8, 1914, CBS-WPW.

46. John A. Lomax to Webb, Austin, Tex., April 30, 1914; Folklore Society of Texas, program of the fourth annual meeting, Austin, Tex., May 9, 1914, CBS-WPW.

47. Franz Boas to Webb, New York, N.Y., October 22, 1915, CBS-WPW.

48. Webb to My dear Janey, Cuero, Tex., October 26, 1915, CBS-WPW.

49. Franz Boas to Webb, New York, N.Y., November 5, 1915, CBS-WPW.

50. Webb to My dearest Sweetheart Jean, Cuero, Tex., November 8, 1915, CBS-WPW.

51. Webb to My Sweetheart Janey, Cuero, Tex., November 4, 1915, CBS-WPW.

52. Webb to Dear Miss Oliphant, Beeville, Tex., August 12, 1913; to My Sweetheart Jean, San Marcos, Tex., November 29, 1914, CBS-WPW. Webb roomed at 1714 Lavaca Street, and the Oliphants owned the house at 1716. T. H. Shelby was long associated with the university's Division of Extension.

53. Webb to My dear Jean, San Marcos, Tex., November 8, 1914, CBS-WPW.

54. Webb to My dear Janey, Cuero, Tex., September 20, 1915, CBS-WPW.

55. H. W. Harper, dean of the Graduate Department, University of Texas, to Webb, Austin, Tex., May 12, 1914, CBS-WPW.

56. "Council Makes Announcement of Fellowships," *The Texan*, no. 175, clipping undated but ca. May 5, 1914, CBS-WPW. Webb was one of eight receiving a scholarship.

57. Webb to My dear Jean, San Antonio, Tex., November 26, 1914, CBS-WPW.

58. Webb to C. E. Evans, Beeville, Tex., May 24, 1914; to My dear Jean, Beeville, Tex., May 30, 1914, CBS-WPW.

59. Webb to My dear Jean, San Marcos, Tex., September 20, November 30, 1914, CBS-WPW.

60. Webb to My dear Jean, San Marcos, Tex., September 20, 1914, CBS-WPW.

61. Webb to My dear Jean, San Marcos, Tex., September 25, 1914, CBS-WPW.

62. Webb to My dear Jean, San Marcos, Tex., October 14, 1914, CBS-WPW.

63. Webb to My dearest Jean, San Marcos, Tex., November 6, 1914, CBS-WPW.

64. Webb to My dear Jean, San Marcos, Tex., September 27, 1914; to My Sweetheart Jean, San Marcos, Tex., November 29, 1914, CBS-WPW. Dr. William J. Battle was acting president of the university. H. Y. Benedict was dean of the College of Arts and Sciences and later president; like Webb, he was from Stephens County. John A. Lomax, the noted folklorist, was secretary of the university.

65. Webb to My dear Jean, San Antonio, Tex., November 26, 1914, CBS-WPW.

66. [Walter Prescott Webb], "Dr. Webb's Last Writing," *Texas Libraries* 25 (Fall 1963): 101.

67. Webb to the Honorable Board of Trustees, San Marcos, Tex., March 31, 1915, CBS-WPW.

68. A. S. Bush to Webb, telegram, Cuero, Tex., May 22, 1915, CBS-WPW.

69. Webb to My dear Janey, Cuero, Tex., September 5, 1915, CBS-WPW.

70. Webb to My dear Janey, Cuero, Tex., September 3, 1915, CBS-WPW.

71. Webb to My dear Janey, Cuero, Tex., September 5, 1915, CBS-WPW.

72. Webb to My dear Jean, San Marcos, Tex., September 25, 1914, CBS-WPW.

73. Webb to My dear Janey, Yorktown, Tex., September 6, 1915; Cuero, Tex., September 10, 1915, CBS-WPW.

74. Webb to My dear Janey, Cuero, Tex., September 10, 22, 1915, CBS-WPW.

75. Webb to My dear Janey, Cuero, Tex., September 12, 13, 1915, CBS-WPW.

76. Webb to My dear Janey, Cuero, Tex., March 16, 1916; Victoria, Tex., March 30, 1916, CBS-WPW.

77. Webb to My dear Janey, Cuero, Tex., September 30, 1915, May 18, 23, 1916, CBS-WPW.

78. Webb to My dear Janey, Cuero, Tex., October 16, December 6, 1915, January 26, February 16, 22, March 12, 16, 21, 1916, CBS-WPW.

79. Webb to My dear Janey, Cuero, Tex., January 27, 1916, CBS-WPW.

80. Webb to My dear Janey, Cuero, Tex., September 23, 1915, CBS-WPW.

81. Webb to My dear Jean, Cuero, Tex., October 9, 1915, CBS-WPW.

82. Webb to My dear Janey, Cuero, Tex., September 14, 1915, CBS-WPW.

83. Webb to My dearest Sweetheart Jean, Cuero, Tex., September 19, 1915, CBS-WPW.

84. TSTA, program of the thirty-seventh annual meeting, Corpus Christi, Tex., November 25–27, 1915, CBS-WPW.

85. Webb to My dear Janey, Cuero, Tex., October 24, 1915, CBS-WPW.

86. Webb to My dear Janey, Cuero, Tex., November 1, 2, 10, 21, 22, 1915, CBS-WPW.

87. Webb to My dear Sweetheart Janey, Corpus Christi, Tex., November 26, 1915, CBS-WPW.

88. "Increasing the Functional Value of History by the Problem Method of Presentation," *History Teacher's Magazine* 7 (May 1916): 155–163.

89. Joe B. Frantz, "Walter Prescott Webb: The Life of a Texan," *Texas Libraries* 25 (Fall 1963): 78.

90. A. W. Birdwell to Webb, Nashville, Tenn., December 4, 1915, January 30, 1916, CBS-WPW.

91. Webb to My dear Janey, Madison, Wis., July 3, 1916, undated notes with this letter, CBS-WPW.

92. Jean to My dearest Walter, Austin, Tex., July 9, 1916, CBS-WPW.

93. Webb to My dear Janey, Cuero, Tex., November 1, 1915, CBS-WPW.

94. Webb to My dear Janey, Cuero, Tex., October 12, December 4, 1915, CBS-WPW.

95. Webb to My dearest sweetheart Jean, Cuero, Tex., November 12, 1915, CBS-WPW.

96. Webb to My dear Janey, Cuero, Tex., May 17, 1916, CBS-WPW.

97. W. G. Rohre to Webb, Lockhart, Tex., May 3, 1916, CBS-WPW.

98. E. M. Schiwetz to the author, College Station, Tex., December 12, 1974.

99. Webb to My dearest Jean, Ranger, Tex., June 27, July 13, 1915, CBS-WPW.

100. Webb to My sweetheart Jean, Cuero, Tex., September 27, 29, October 5, 1915, CBS-WPW.

101. Webb to My dear Janey, Cuero, Tex., October 25, November 28, December 1, 1915, March 20, 1916, CBS-WPW.

102. Webb to My dear Janey, Cuero, Tex., March 31, April 13, 14, 18, 25, 1916, CBS-WPW.

103. Omri F. Hibbard to Webb, New York, N.Y., September 30, December 3, 1915, March 9, April 17, 1916; Ida K. Hinds to Dear Friend, New York, N.Y., January 14, February 1, 3, 9, March 20, 1916; Aunt Ida to Walter, Los Angeles, Cal., April 5, 1917, CBS-WPW.

104. Webb to My sweet Janey, Cuero, Tex., February 15, 1916; to My dear Janey, Cuero, Tex., February 27, 1916, CBS-WPW.

105. Webb to My dear Janey, Cuero, Tex., February 27, March 22, 1916, CBS-WPW.

106. Webb to My dear Janey, Cuero, Tex., March 12, 1916, CBS-WPW.

107. *Texas History Teachers' Bulletin*, University of Texas Bulletin no. 1864, November 15, 1918, pp. 7–13.

108. Autobiography, Walter Prescott Webb Papers, box 2M245, p. 127, University of Texas Archives, Austin (hereafter referred to as WP); [Webb], "Dr. Webb's Last Writing," pp. 96–100.

109. Frederic Duncalf to Webb, Austin, Tex., March 24, 1918, WP, box 2M257.

110. Autobiography, WP, box 2M245, p. 130.

111. The actual appointment came through Professor Eugene C. Barker's letter to President Robert E. Vinson, October 30, 1918, and F. W. Gaff's letter to Barker, November 1, 1918. The appointment was effective November 1, 1918, at a salary of $1,600 (Barker Papers A1/134, University of Texas Archives, Austin).

112. "The Historical Seminar: Its Outer Shell and Its Inner Spirit," *Mississippi Valley Historical Review* 42 (June 1955): 3–23.

113. Walter Rundell, Jr., *Walter Prescott Webb* (Austin: Steck-Vaughn, 1971), pp. 7–22.